Ric Pimentel
Terry Wall

Cambridge
checkpoint

NEW EDITION

checkp●int
Maths

2

Workbook

HODDER
EDUCATION
AN HACHETTE UK COMPANY

Hachette UK's policy is to use papers that are natural, renewable and recyclable products and made from wood grown in sustainable forests. The logging and manufacturing processes are expected to conform to the environmental regulations of the country of origin.

Orders: please contact Bookpoint Ltd, 130 Milton Park, Abingdon, Oxon OX14 4SB. Telephone: (44) 01235 827720. Fax: (44) 01235 400454. Lines are open 9.00–5.00, Monday to Saturday, with a 24-hour message answering service. Visit our website at www.hoddereducation.co.uk

© Ric Pimentel and Terry Wall 2012
First published in 2012 by
Hodder Education, an Hachette UK Company,
338 Euston Road
London NW1 3BH

Impression number   5 4 3
Year   2016 2015 2014 2013

Cover photo © Macduff Everton/CORBIS
Typeset in Palatino 10.5/12.5 by Pantek Media, Maidstone, Kent
Printed in the UK

A catalogue record for this title is available from the British Library

ISBN 978 1444 144 031

Contents

	SECTION 1	1
Chapter 1	Place value, ordering and rounding	1
Chapter 2	Expressions, equations and formulae	9
Chapter 3	Congruency and properties of two-dimensional shapes	13
Chapter 4	Measures and motion	18
Chapter 5	Collecting and displaying data	25
Chapter 6	Calculations and mental strategies 1	32
	SECTION 2	**36**
Chapter 8	Integers, powers and roots	36
Chapter 9	Equations and simple functions	42
Chapter 10	Constructions	51
Chapter 11	Transformations	54
Chapter 12	Statistical calculations	58
Chapter 13	Calculations and mental strategies 2	62
	SECTION 3	**67**
Chapter 15	Fractions, decimals and percentages	67
Chapter 16	Sequences, functions and graphs	75
Chapter 17	Angle properties	83
Chapter 18	Area and volume	88
Chapter 19	Interpreting data and graphs	97
Chapter 20	Calculations and mental strategies 3	102
	SECTION 4	**107**
Chapter 22	Ratio and proportion	107
Chapter 23	Formulae and substitution	115
Chapter 24	Enlargement and scale drawing	120
Chapter 25	Nets and surface area	126
Chapter 26	Probability	128
Chapter 27	Calculations and mental strategies 4	133

SECTION 1

1 Place value, ordering and rounding

Place value and the decimal number system

Exercise 1.1

1 Write each of the following numbers in words.

   a) 11 327 _____

   b) 83 348 _____

   c) 134 850 000 _____

Rounding

To **round** a number, look at the next digit after the one in question. If that digit is 5 or more, round up. If it is 4 or less, round down.

Example 1:   8 794 000 to the nearest million is 9 million.

Example 2:   9.456 to the nearest whole number is 9, to one decimal place is 9.5, and to two decimal places is 9.46.

Sometimes you may need to use common sense in deciding whether to round up or round down.

Example 3:   A sign saying 'Maximum height 7 m' on a bridge 6.7 m high is not helpful. A lorry that is 6.8 m high would crash.

Exercise 1.2

1   Round each of these numbers to the degree of accuracy shown in brackets.

   a) 7765   (nearest hundred) _____

   b) 1099   (nearest thousand) _____

   c) 487   (nearest ten) _____

   d) 34 766   (nearest hundred) _____

   e) 45 620 000   (nearest million) _____

2   A survey showed that 11 327 cars were loaded onto a company's ferries on one Sunday.
   Round this number **a)** to the nearest ten, **b)** to the nearest hundred and **c)** to the nearest thousand.

   a) _____   **b)** _____   **c)** _____

3   A school hall holds 269 people.
   Round this number to the nearest hundred.

   _____

4   The rock band U2 played in front of 83 348 people in England.
   Round this number to the nearest thousand.

   _____

5   From London to New York is 5267 km.
   Round this distance to the nearest 100 km.

   _____

6   A stadium was built at a cost of $134 850 000.
   Round this amount to the nearest $ million.

   _____

7 The top table gives the exact distances (in kilometres) between some cities in Europe. In the blank spaces in the bottom table write each distance to the nearest 100 km.

	Copenhagen	Edinburgh	Frankfurt	Geneva
Copenhagen	—	1864	799	1531
Edinburgh	1864	—	1395	1536
Frankfurt	799	1395	—	585
Geneva	1531	1536	585	—

	Copenhagen	Edinburgh	Frankfurt	Geneva
Copenhagen	—			
Edinburgh		—		
Frankfurt			—	
Geneva				—

8 Round each of the following numbers **(i)** to the nearest whole number, **(ii)** to one decimal place and **(iii)** to two decimal places.

a) 8.754

(i) _____ (ii) _____ (iii) _____

b) 7.487

(i) _____ (ii) _____ (iii) _____

c) 18.295

(i) _____ (ii) _____ (iii) _____

d) 0.1436

(i) _____ (ii) _____ (iii) _____

e) 5.756

(i) _____ (ii) _____ (iii) _____

f) 9.987

(i) _____ (ii) _____ (iii) _____

g) 19.3654

(i) _____ (ii) _____ (iii) _____

h) 9.2978

(i) _____ (ii) _____ (iii) _____

i) 14.5656

(i) _____ (ii) _____ (iii) _____

j) 0.6788

(i) _____ (ii) _____ (iii) _____

9 A stadium has 54 790 seats. What would you say was its maximum capacity:

a) to the nearest thousand? _____

b) to the nearest hundred? _____

10 A bridge is to be built over a river 1245 m wide.
Write down a sensible estimate of its length, to a whole 100 m, for working out how much steel will be needed.

_____

11 A truck can safely carry a weight of 18.4 tonnes.
What is its maximum load to a whole number of tonnes?

_____

12 A pilot needs to know the maximum height an aircraft can fly at. The cabin has been tested and is safe to a height of 15 679 m.
Round this height appropriately:

a) to a whole number of kilometres _____

b) to a whole 100 m. _____

13 A submarine can work safely to a depth of 2067.3 metres.
What is its safe working depth to a whole number of metres?

_____

14 A car transporter can carry 12 cars.
How many transporters are needed for 67 cars?

_____

15 Holiday caravans are being sited on a concrete base. Each base needs 450 kg of
concrete. A cement truck carries 10 tonnes of concrete.
How many bases can be laid from one truck-load of concrete?

_____

16 Each caravan is surrounded by a hedge of 18 trees.
How many caravans can be surrounded using 2000 trees?

_____

17 A ship can carry 18 000 tonnes of cargo. A full container weighs 11 tonnes.
How many containers can the ship carry safely?

_____

18 A plane can carry 12.7 tonnes of cargo. A full container weighs 1.8 tonnes.
How many containers can the plane carry safely?

_____

19 A baker makes loaves weighing 500 g.
How many loaves can he make from 3.9 kg of dough?

_____

20 School classrooms are being built on a concrete base. Each room's base needs
650 kg of concrete. A cement truck carries 18 tonnes of concrete.
How many bases can be laid from one truck-load of concrete?

_____

Multiplying and dividing integers by 0.1 and 0.01

Multiplying by 0.1 is the same as multiplying by $\frac{1}{10}$ and as dividing by 10.

Multiplying by 0.01 is the same as multiplying by $\frac{1}{100}$ and as dividing by 100.

Example 1: $10.2 \times 0.1 = 10.2 \div 10 = 1.02$

Example 2: $3460 \times 0.01 = 3460 \div 100 = 34.6$

Dividing by 0.1 is the same as dividing by $\frac{1}{10}$ and as multiplying by 10.

Dividing by 0.01 is the same as dividing by $\frac{1}{100}$ and as multiplying by 100.

Example 3: $9.3 \div 0.1 = 9.3 \times 10 = 93$

Example 4: $4.62 \div 0.01 = 4.62 \times 100 = 462$

Exercise 1.3

1   Work out the following multiplications without using a calculator.

   a) $160 \times 0.1 =$ _____   **b)** $250 \times 0.1 =$ _____

   c) $2260 \times 0.1 =$ _____   **d)** $1200 \times 0.1 =$ _____

   e) $6760 \times 0.1 =$ _____   **f)** $3960 \times 0.01 =$ _____

   g) $6350 \times 0.01 =$ _____   **h)** $9200 \times 0.01 =$ _____

   i) $60 \times 0.01 =$ _____   **j)** $5 \times 0.01 =$ _____

2   Work out the following divisions without using a calculator.

   a) $1.9 \div 0.1 =$ _____   **b)** $34.2 \div 0.1 =$ _____

   c) $0.2 \div 0.1 =$ _____   **d)** $0.37 \div 0.1 =$ _____

   e) $13.03 \div 0.1 =$ _____   **f)** $45.82 \div 0.01 =$ _____

   g) $0.43 \div 0.01 =$ _____

3 A 10 cent coin is worth $0.10.
How many 10 cent coins are there in $4.50?

_____

4 A piece of wood 6 m 20 cm long is marked off into 0.1 m lengths.
How many 0.1 m lengths are there?

_____

5 A truck travels 0.72 km on 0.01 litre of fuel.
How many kilometres will it travel on 1 litre of fuel?

_____

Inequalities

When two values are equal we use the sign = to show this. We can write inequalities using the signs > (is greater than) and < (is less than).

Exercise 1.4

1 Write one of the symbols =, > or <, to make each of these statements true.

   a) 5×4 _____ 7×3 **b)** $6 + 6$ _____ 4×3

   c) $8 + 7$ _____ 4×4 **d)** 90 cm _____ 1 m

   e) 80 cm _____ 0.7 m   **f)** 100 cm _____ 1000 mm

   g) 1 m _____ 100 cm   **h)** 3 tonnes _____ 3500 kg

   i) $5 \times 5 \times 5$ _____ 25×5 **j)** 8×0.01 _____ $0.8 \div 10$

→

2 Write each of the following sets of numbers in order of size, smallest first. Use the symbol for 'less than' in your answers.

a) 0.7,   0.6,   0.8,   0.09,   1,   0.99

_____

b) 0.66,   6.6,   6,   6.3,   0.6,   0.06

_____

c) 2,   2.4,   0.22,   0.42,   4,   0.024

_____

d) 1.6,   0.16,   11.6,   1.66,   1.06,   1.066

_____

e) 8.3,   7.3,   7.33,   8.33,   7.03,   8.333

_____

Teacher comments

2 Expressions, equations and formulae

An **expression** represents a value in algebraic form. In the expression $4x - 6$, $4x$ and -6 are **terms** in the expression.

An **equation** contains an equals sign (=) and shows that the expressions either side of it have the same value. In the equation $4x - 6 = 2x + 4$, the expression $4x - 6$ has the same value as the expression $2x + 4$. The equation can be **solved** to find the value of the unknown quantity x (the variable) that makes it correct.

A **formula** (plural formulae) describes a relationship between different variables. The formula $A = l \times w$ describes the relationship between the area (A) of a rectangle and its length (l) and width (w).

The number value of the expression $4x - 6$ depends on the value of the variable x. It is a **function** of x. We can write $f(x) = 4x - 6$.

Exercise 2.0

1   Give an example of an expression and an equation.
    What is the difference between them?

    Expression _____   Equation _____

    _____

    _____

2   What is a formula? Give two examples, with a diagram for one of them.

    _____ _____

3   Use a mapping diagram to show what is meant by a function.

Constructing expressions

Some expressions contain a number of terms. Sometimes the expression can be simplified by collecting together the **like terms**.

Example: $2a + 5c + a - c = 3a + 4c$

Exercise 2.1

1 Simplify the following expressions.

    a) $3a - 5a + 4a =$ _____

    b) $3b - 8 + 4b + 4 =$ _____

    c) $6c + 9 - 4c + 11 + c =$ _____

    d) $7d - 3d + 9 - 5d =$ _____

    e) $8 + 4e - 8e - 3 =$ _____

    f) $5f + 3 - 7f - 4 =$ _____

    g) $9g - 5 - g + 4g - 8 =$ _____

    h) $-3h - 3h - 3h - 3h =$ _____

    i) $4i + 4i - 4i - 4i + 1 =$ _____

    j) $-7j + 3j - 2j + 8j =$ _____

2 Write a formula for the perimeter P of each of these shapes.

a)

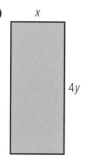

$P =$ _____

b)

$P =$ _____

c)

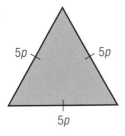

$P =$ _____

d)

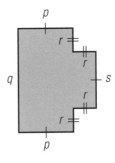

$P =$ _____

e)

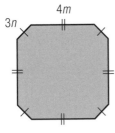

$P =$ _____

Expressions with brackets

To **expand** brackets, multiply the terms inside the brackets by the term outside.

Example 1: $2(x + 5) = 2 \times x + 2 \times 5 = 2x + 10$

Example 2: $-5a(3b + 2c - 6) = -15ab - 10ac + 30a$

Exercise 2.2

Expand the brackets in these expressions and simplify your answer where possible.

1 $3(5 - a) =$ _____

2 $2a(2b + 3) =$ _____

3 $4b(7 + 3c) - 2 =$ _____

4 $6(d - 2) - 2(d + 2) = $ _____

5 $(e - 3) - 4(2e + 1) = $ _____

6 $(f - 1) - (f - 1) + 1 = $ _____

7 $2(7 - 9g) - 3(4 - 2g) = $ _____

8 $5a(6 + 2b) + 6ab - 7 = $ _____

9 $2x(3y - 1) + 2x(3y + 1) = $ _____

10 $6p(q + 9) - 3p(2q - 1) = $ _____

Teacher comments

Congruency and properties of two-dimensional shapes

3

Congruency

Two shapes are **congruent** if they are exactly the same shape and size.
Two triangles are congruent if they meet any of the following sets of conditions:

- side, side, side (SSS)
- side, angle, side (SAS)
- angle, angle, side (AAS)
- angle, side, angle (ASA)
- right angle, hypotenuse, side (RHS).

Exercise 3.1

1   Which of these shapes are congruent to shape A?

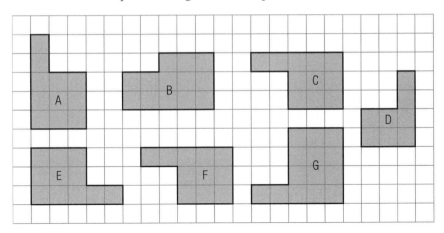

→

2 From the information given, determine whether these triangles *must* be congruent. Give reasons for your answer.

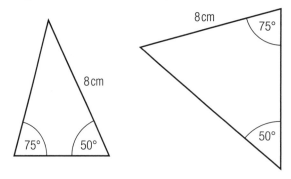

Congruent? _____

Reasons _____

_____

Properties of quadrilaterals

A **quadrilateral** is any closed two-dimensional shape with four straight sides.

Exercise 3.2

What special name is given to each of the following quadrilaterals?

1 All sides equal in length and two pairs of opposite angles equal

_____

2 One pair of parallel sides

_____

3 Two pairs of opposite sides equal in length and two pairs of opposite angles equal

_____

4 One pair of opposite angles equal

_____

Symmetry properties of two-dimensional shapes

A shape has **reflection symmetry** if it looks the same on both sides of a mirror line. A shape has **rotational symmetry** if, during one complete revolution of 360° about the **centre of rotation**, it looks the same as the shape in its original position.

Exercise 3.3

1   Complete this table of the symmetry properties of different types of shapes.

Shape		Number of lines of symmetry	Order of rotational symmetry
Square			
Rhombus			
Isosceles trapezium			
Kite			
Equilateral triangle			
Regular hexagon			
Circle			

→

2 For each of these capital letters:

   (i) draw the lines of reflection symmetry

   (ii) write down the order of rotational symmetry.

a) **D**   b) **H**   c) **O**   d) **T**

Order = _____   Order = _____   Order = _____   Order = _____

3 Complete each of the following diagrams by drawing in additional lines so that the final shape has the symmetry stated.

a)

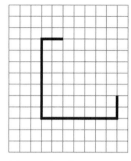

1 line of reflection symmetry

Rotational symmetry of order 1

b)

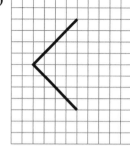

4 lines of reflection symmetry

Rotational symmetry of order 4

c)

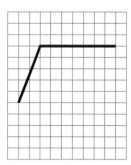

0 lines of reflection symmetry

Rotational symmetry of order 2

d)

1 line of reflection symmetry

Rotational symmetry of order 0

4 In each of the 3 × 4 grids below, shade in squares so that the final shape has the symmetry stated.

a)

b)

2 lines of reflection symmetry

Rotational symmetry of order 2

0 lines of reflection symmetry

Rotational symmetry of order 2

Teacher comments

4 Measures and motion

The metric system

The metric units for **length** are:

> kilometre (km), metre (m), centimetre (cm) and millimetre (mm)

The metric units for **mass** are:

> tonne (t), kilogram (kg), gram (g) and milligram (mg)

The metric units for **capacity** are:

> litre (l) and millilitre (ml)

We can use the units for length to convert between different units of area.
Example: $1\,cm = 10\,mm$ so $1\,cm^2 = 10\,mm \times 10\,mm = 100\,mm^2$

Exercise 4.1

1   Complete the following.

a) There are _____ millimetres in 9 metres.

b) There are _____ centimetres in 7.5 metres.

c) There are _____ grams in 3.55 kilograms.

d) There are _____ metres in 1.452 kilometres.

e) There are _____ millilitres in 7.56 litres.

f) There are _____ kilograms in 3.78 tonnes.

g) $25\,cm^2 =$ _____ mm^2 h) $5\,m^2 =$ _____ cm^2

i) _____ $m^2 = 800\,000\,cm^2$ j) _____ $cm^2 = 2\,m^2$

2 Write an estimate for each of the following using a sensible unit.

a) the width of your foot _____

b) the amount of water in a lake _____

c) the mass of a girl _____

d) the capacity of the fuel tanks of a plane _____

e) the length of your thigh bone _____

f) the capacity of a large glass _____

g) the distance to the nearest city _____

h) the mass of a bus _____

i) the width of the River Amazon _____

j) the distance to the nearest star _____

✪ **3** Complete the following.

a) $1 \text{cm}^2 =$ _____ mm^2 b) $1 \text{m}^2 =$ _____ cm^2

c) _____ $\text{m}^2 = 2\,500\,000 \text{mm}^2$ d) $4000 \text{cm}^2 =$ _____ m^2

e) _____ $\text{cm}^2 = 7500 \text{mm}^2$

4 Write an estimate for each of the following using a sensible unit.
Show how you arrived at your answers.
a) the area of the school site

_____

_____

→

b) the area of a piece of writing paper

_____

_____

c) the volume of a large box

_____

_____

d) the height of a house

_____

_____

e) the area of your country

_____

_____

Imperial units

In some countries, **imperial units** are used as measures of distance.

1760 yards = 1 mile   and   1 yard = 3 feet

Rough conversions between imperial and metric units are as follows.

1 metre = 1.093 613 298 yards, or about 1.1 yards.
1 yard = 0.9144 m, or about 0.9 m.
1 km = 0.621 371 192 237 mile, or about 0.6 mile or $\frac{5}{8}$ mile.

1 mile = 1.609 34 km, or about 1.6 km or $\frac{8}{5}$ km.

Exercise 4.2

1 Convert each length or distance into the units shown.
Use the following conversions.
$1\,km = \frac{5}{8}$ mile and 1 mile $= \frac{8}{5}\,km$.

1760 yards = 1 mile.
1 yard = 3 feet.
1 yard = 0.9 m and 1 m = 1.1 yard.

Give your answers to the nearest whole number.

a) 5.2 miles = _____ km

b) 400 m = _____ yards

c) 330 feet = _____ yards

d) 9900 feet = _____ m

e) 10000 m = _____ miles

f) 800 m = _____ yards

g) 6 feet = _____ cm

h) 100000 miles = _____ km

i) 20 km = _____ feet

2 A plane is flying at 28000 feet. What is its height in metres?

_____

3 A man is 6 feet tall. What is his height in centimetres?

_____

4 Mount Everest is 29102 feet high. What is its height in metres?

_____

5 The distance from London to New York is 3450 miles.
What is the distance in kilometres?

_____

6 A marathon run is 26 miles 365 yards. What is the distance in metres?

_____

7 An Olympic triple jumper jumped 28.5 feet. What is the length in metres?

_____

8 A javelin is thrown 132.4 metres. What is the distance in yards?

_____

9 A football field is 70 metres wide. What is the width in yards?

_____

10 The Moon is 260 000 miles from Earth. What is the distance in kilometres?

_____

Travel graphs

The motion of an object can be displayed on a **distance–time graph**. If an object is travelling at constant speed, the distance–time graph is a straight line. For example, the graph below.

Example: This distance–time graph shows that the object moves 240 m in 60 s.
The speed is $\frac{240}{60} = 4$ m/s.

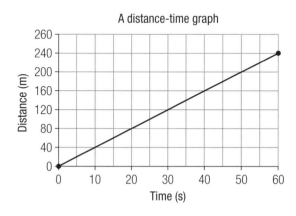

A distance-time graph

Exercise 4.3

1 Here is a description of a woman's walk.

- She sets off at 8.30a.m. and walks at a constant speed of 4 km/h.
- She stops at 9.30a.m. for a half-hour rest.
- After her rest she walks a further 6 km at a constant speed, stopping again at 11.30a.m.
- At 11.30a.m. she stops for half an hour before setting off again at a constant speed of 5 km/h.
- She arrives at her destination at 2.00p.m.

Plot a distance–time graph to show the woman's trip.

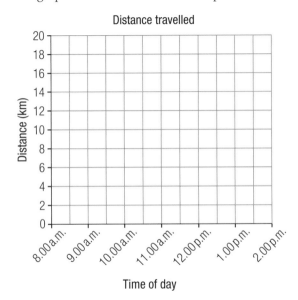

→

2 A distance–time graph is plotted to represent a train's journey, showing its distance *from its starting point*.
Explain, giving reasons, whether or not each of the graphs below can possibly represent the motion of the train.

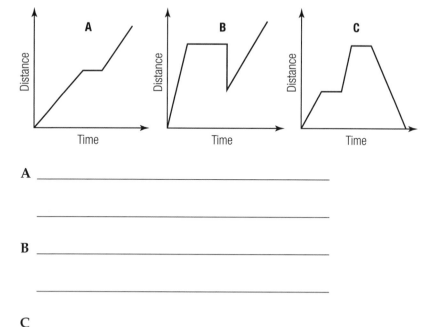

A _____

_____

B _____

_____

C _____

_____

Teacher comments

Collecting and displaying data

Discrete and continuous data

Quantitative data, that is data that can be measured, falls into two categories: **discrete** and **continuous** data. Discrete data can only take specific values. Continuous data can take any value (usually within a range).

Exercise 5.1

Write either 'discrete' or 'continuous' to describe each of the following types of data.

1   The mass of a suitcase (kg) _____

2   The temperature of an oven (°C) _____

3   The number of cars in a car park _____

4   The volume of a container (cm^3) _____

Collecting data

Data is often collected in response to a problem. One method is to **interview** people; another method is to use **questionnaires**.
Usually it is not possible to interview a whole 'population' so a **sample** is used. The size of the sample depends on factors such as time and cost.

Exercise 5.2

1   **a)** Give one advantage of interviewing as a method of data collection.

    _____

    b) Give one disadvantage of interviewing as a method of data collection.

    _____

→

2   **a)** Give one advantage of questionnaires as a method of data collection.

_____

b) Give one disadvantage of questionnaires as a method of data collection.

_____

3   Here are some questions for a questionnaire about students' health.
Explain what is wrong with each question.
a) How old are you?
    11–12 ☐   12–13 ☐   13–14 ☐

_____

_____

b) Are you healthy?
    Yes ☐   No ☐

_____

_____

c) Being healthy is important. Do you agree?
    Yes ☐   No ☐   Not sure ☐

_____

_____

Displaying data

Once the data has been collected, it can be displayed in different ways, including
two-way tables, **frequency tables** and **diagrams**, **histograms**, **pie charts**, **stem-and-leaf diagrams** and **line graphs**.

Exercise 5.3

1   This two-way table shows the numbers of people participating in different sports during one day at a sports centre.

	Sport				
	Football	Tennis	Badminton	Squash	Swimming
Men	43	8	12	16	25
Women	4	22	18	4	45
Boys	38	26	5	10	16
Girls	6	30	18	2	41

a) How many people played squash on that day?

_____

b) How many women did sport at the sports centre on that day?

_____

c) How many girls did swimming?

_____

d) How many more women than men played tennis?

_____

2   This data records the masses (in kilograms) of 25 students.

48   52   42   38   46   51   50   47   45   40   37   46   49
50   52   61   53   45   39   40   42   51   38   55   46

a) Enter the data in the grouped tally and frequency table.

Mass (kg)	Tally	Frequency
$35 \leqslant M < 40$		
$40 \leqslant M < 45$		
$45 \leqslant M < 50$		
$50 \leqslant M < 55$		
$55 \leqslant M < 60$		
$60 \leqslant M < 65$		

b) Draw a histogram of the grouped results.

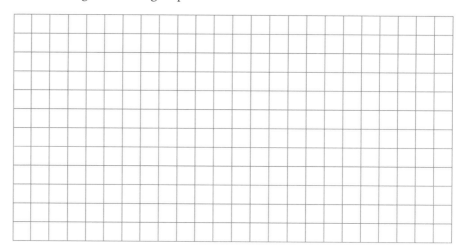

3   This table shows the favourite ice-creams of 40 children.

Flavour	Vanilla	Chocolate	Strawberry	Mint	Toffee	Other
Frequency	7	12	8	4	3	6

a) What fraction of the total number of children prefer each flavour?

Flavour	Vanilla	Chocolate	Strawberry	Mint	Toffee	Other
Fraction						

b) Write each fraction as a percentage and as an angle (out of a total of 360°).

Flavour	Vanilla	Chocolate	Strawberry	Mint	Toffee	Other
Percentage						
Angle						

c) Draw a pie chart to show the data.

4   The table shows the numbers of different types of coffee sold in a coffee shop.

Coffee	Espresso	Latte	Cappuccino	Filter	Other
Frequency	15	20	30	10	5
Fraction					
Percentage					
Angle					

a) Complete the table.

b) Draw a pie chart to show the data.

5   A weather report lists the following depths of snow (in centimetres) in different parts of a country.

   8   12   18   11   25   42   33   12   15   18   18
   6   22   28   31   32   44   24   31   17   9   10
   11   23   33   11

a) Draw a stem-and-leaf diagram to show the data.

b) From your diagram deduce:

(i) the modal depth of snow _____

(ii) the mean depth of snow. _____

c) (i) Ring the median data value (or the median pair of values) on the stem-and-leaf diagram.

(ii) Write down the median depth of snow. _____

6   The number of people in a swimming pool is recorded every hour on one particular day. The results are shown in the table.

Time	9 00	10 00	11 00	12 00	13 00	14 00	15 00	16 00	17 00	18 00	19 00
Number of people	5	8	15	32	28	20	12	13	18	25	40

a) Draw a line graph to show the number of people in the pool during the day.

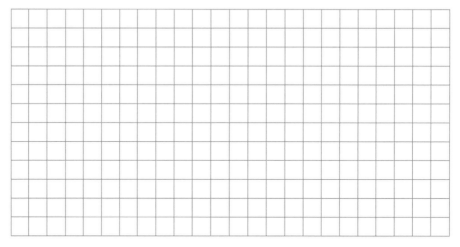

b) From your graph estimate the number of people in the pool at 11 30.

_____

c) Explain why your answer to part **b)** is only an estimate.

_____

d) Estimate the amount of time during the day when there were more than 25 people in the pool. Show your method clearly on the graph.

_____

Teacher comments

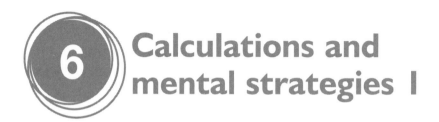

Calculations and mental strategies 1

Mental strategies

Exercise 6.1

Do these questions in your head, without using a calculator.

1 a) $5 \times 5 \times 5 = $ _____ b) $3 \times 3 \times 3 = $ _____

2 a) $9 \times 9 = $ _____ b) $4 \times 4 = $ _____

3 a) $7 \times 7 = $ _____ b) $8 \times 8 = $ _____

4 a) $10 \times 10 = $ _____ b) $12 \times 12 = $ _____

5 a) $11 \times 11 = $ _____ b) $13 \times 13 = $ _____

6 a) $15 \times 15 = $ _____ b) $17 \times 17 = $ _____

7 a) $2 \times 2 \times 2 = $ _____ b) $14 \times 14 = $ _____

8 a) $1 \times 1 \times 1 = $ _____ b) $4 \times 4 \times 4 = $ _____

9 a) $6 \times 6 \times 6 = $ _____ b) $9 \times 9 \times 9 = $ _____

10 a) $16 \times 16 = $ _____ b) $19 \times 19 = $ _____

11 Convert these to millimetres.

   a) 7 cm _____ b) 1.2 cm _____

12 Convert these to metres.

   a) 450 cm _____ b) 900 cm _____

13 Convert these to kilometres.

a) 5000 m _____

b) 6000 m _____

14 Complete these sentences.

a) To change kg to g _____

b) To change g to kg _____

15 Convert these to kilograms.

a) 2 tonnes _____

b) 2.2 tonnes _____

c) 10 000 g _____

d) 3000 g _____

16 Convert these to millilitres.

a) 1.5 litres _____

b) 1.4 litres _____

c) 3.2 litres _____

d) 1.75 litres _____

17 Convert these to litres.

a) 3400 m*l* _____

b) 1200 m*l* _____

c) 12 m*l* _____

d) 850 m*l* _____

Using a calculator

Exercise 6.2

Use a calculator to work out the answers to the following calculations.

1 **a)** 9.1 − 7.4 = _____

b) 8.9 − 6.8 = _____

c) 21.1 − 16.05 = _____

➡

CHAPTER 6

2 **a)** $-7.4 + 5.55 =$ _____

   b) $-6.1 + 11.5 =$ _____

   c) $-6.35 - 7.8 =$ _____

3 **a)** $-13.3 - 13.33 =$ _____

   b) $-4 - 10.4 =$ _____

   c) $-12 - 22.4 =$ _____

4 **a)** $-52.9 - (-65) =$ _____

   b) $-13.56 - (-24.23) =$ _____

   c) $-4 - (-12.85) =$ _____

5 **a)** $34.6 \times 13.7 =$ _____

   b) $14.2 \times 38.3 =$ _____

   c) $15.5 \times 43.6 \times 62.2 =$ _____

   d) $212.4 \times 23.1 =$ _____

   e) $87.02 \times -45 =$ _____

6 **a)** $18 \times 3 + 36 =$ _____

   b) $34 + 10 \times 62 =$ _____

   c) $66 - 38 \div 19 =$ _____

   d) $144 - 124 \div 4 =$ _____

   e) $39 \times 6 \div 18 =$ _____

7 **a)** $4 + 3 \times 2 - 3 = $ _____

   b) $7 - 6 \div 3 + 5 = $ _____

   c) $50 \div 5 \times 2 - 38 = $ _____

   d) $16 - 16 \div 8 + 2 \times 4 = $ _____

   e) $5 + 5 \times 12 \div 6 - 5 = $ _____

8 **a)** $3^2 + 4 - 12 = $ _____

   b) $24 + 8^2 - 3^3 = $ _____

   c) $12 - \dfrac{6^3}{16 + 2} = $ _____

   d) $\dfrac{(5 + 3)^2}{6 - 1} - 7 = $ _____

   e) $\dfrac{4^3 + 6^2}{2^5} - 3 \times 5 = $ _____

9 **a)** $(40 - 8) \div 10 + 6 = $ _____

   b) $20 - (8 \div 10) + 6 = $ _____

   c) $(20 - 8) \div (10 + 6) = $ _____

   d) $20 - 8 \div (10 + 6) = $ _____

   e) $20 - 8 \div 10 + 6 = $ _____

Teacher comments

SECTION 2

8 Integers, powers and roots

Integers

Integers are whole numbers, and can be positive, negative or zero. Integers can be added together, subtracted from each other, multiplied and divided.

Example 1: $(-14) - (-4) = -10$
Example 2: $(-9) \times (+50) = -450$
Example 3: $(-24) \div (-3) = +8$

Exercise 8.1

Work out the answers to the calculations in questions 1–5.

1 a) $(+1) + (-7) =$ _____

b) $(+3) + (-9) =$ _____

c) $(+16) + (-16) =$ _____

2 a) $(-6) - (+9) =$ _____

b) $(-14) - (+4) =$ _____

c) $(-12) - (+18) =$ _____

3 a) $(-19) - (-5) =$ _____

b) $(-23) - (-22) =$ _____

c) $(-44) - (-51) =$ _____

4 a) $(+7) \times (-6) =$ _____

b) $(+9) \times (-5) =$ _____

c) $(+6) \times (-7) =$ _____

5 a) $(-8) \times (+4) =$ _____

b) $(-9) \times (+9) =$ _____

c) $(-6) \times (+7) =$ _____

6 Complete this multiplication grid. Some answers are already filled in.

×	−6	−4	−2	0	+2	+4	+6
+3			−6				
+2							
+1	−6						
0		0			0		
−1							−6
−2							
−3							

Work out the answers to the calculations in questions 7–9.

7 **a)** $(+4) \times (+12) =$ _____ **b)** $(-3) \times (+11) =$ _____

c) $(+13) \times (-4) =$ _____

8 **a)** $(-12) \times (-5) =$ _____ **b)** $(-5) \times (-14) =$ _____

c) $(-13) \times (-13) =$ _____

9 **a)** $(+18) \div (+9) =$ _____ **b)** $(+18) \div (-9) =$ _____

c) $(-18) \div (+9) =$ _____ **d)** $(-18) \div (-9) =$ _____

e) $(-24) \div (-8) =$ _____ **f)** $(-20) \div (+5) =$ _____

10 Write in the missing numbers to make each of these calculations correct.

a) _____ $\times (+5) = (+15)$ **b)** _____ $\times (-3) = (-27)$

c) _____ $\times (-5) = (-25)$ **d)** $(-7) \times$ _____ $= (-21)$

e) $(+6) \times$ _____ $= (-48)$ **f)** $(-8) \times$ _____ $= (+64)$

11 The table gives pairs of numbers x and y which add together to make 12.
That is, $x + y = 12$.
Complete the table.

x	+5	+4	+3	+2	+1	0	−1	−2	−3	−4	−5
y											

12 If $p + q = -8$, complete this table.

p	+5	+4	+3	+2	+1	0	−1	−2	−3	−4	−5
q											

13 If $xy = +48$, complete this table. (Remember, xy means x multiplied by y.)

x	+4	+3	+2	+1	−1	−2	−3	−4
y								

Factors, prime numbers and prime factors

The **factors** of a number are all the whole numbers which divide into it exactly.
A **prime number** is a number which has only two factors, 1 and itself.
A **prime factor** is a factor which is also a prime number.

Example 1:   The prime factors of 20 are 2 and 5. $20 = 2 \times 2 \times 5 = 2^2 \times 5$

The **multiples** of a number are the numbers in its times table; these are the numbers which it will divide into exactly. The **common multiples** of two or more numbers are the numbers which are multiples of all of them.
The **highest common factor** (HCF) of two or more numbers is the largest number which is a factor of all of them.

Example 2:   The highest common factor of 14 and 49 is 7.

The **lowest common multiple** (LCM) of two or more numbers is the smallest number which is a multiple of all of them.

Example 3:   The lowest common multiple of 6 and 8 is 24.

Exercise 8.2

1 Find the prime factors of the following numbers. Express each number as a product of prime numbers, using indices when needed.

a) 22

Factors _____

22 = _____ × _____

b) 34

Factors _____

34 = _____
c) 40

Factors _____

40 = _____
d) 128

Factors _____

128 = _____
e) 144

Factors _____

144 = _____

2   Find the highest common factor of the following numbers.

a) 8, 12 _____   **b)** 10, 25 _____

c) 6, 9, 36 _____   **d)** 7, 21, 49 _____

e) 36, 63, 90 _____

3   Find the lowest common multiple of the following numbers.

a) 6, 12 _____   **b)** 4, 11 _____

c) 3, 5, 15 _____   **d)** 3, 5, 10 _____

e) 3, 9, 15 _____

Powers and roots

Squaring a number is multiplying it by itself. The inverse of squaring a number is finding its **square root**. Every positive number has a positive and a negative square root.

Example 1: The square of 7 is $7 \times 7 = 49$.
The square of -7 is $(-7) \times (-7) = 49$.
The square roots of 49 are 7 and -7.

Cubing a number is multiplying it by itself twice. The inverse of cubing a number is finding its **cube root**.

Example 2: The cube of 4 is $4 \times 4 \times 4 = 64$ and $\sqrt[3]{64} = 4$.

A short way to write squares, cubes and other **powers** is to use **index notation**.

Example 3: $6 \times 6 \times 6 = 6^3$

Exercise 8.3

1 Evaluate the following without using a calculator.
Give positive and negative roots.

a) $\sqrt{9}$ _____

b) $\sqrt{81}$ _____

c) $\sqrt{144}$ _____

d) $\sqrt{1}$ _____

e) $\sqrt{0.09}$ _____

f) $\sqrt{0.16}$ _____

2 Evaluate the following without using a calculator.
Give positive and negative roots.

a) $\sqrt{\frac{1}{4}}$ _____

b) $\sqrt{\frac{1}{49}}$ _____

c) $\sqrt{\frac{4}{36}}$ _____

d) $\sqrt{\frac{49}{121}}$ _____

e) $\sqrt{\frac{81}{144}}$ _____

f) $\sqrt{\frac{49}{64}}$ _____

3 Using the $\boxed{y^x}$ button on your calculator, evaluate the following.

a) 7^3 _____

b) 12^3 _____

c) 0.5^3 _____

d) 1.2^3 _____

4 Without using a calculator, work out the cube roots of the following numbers.

a) 27 _____ **b)** 216 _____

c) 8 _____ **d)** 27 000 _____

f) −64 _____ **g)** −1000 _____

h) −343 _____

5 Write each of the following using index notation.

a) $5 \times 5 \times 5 = $ _____

b) $7 \times 7 \times 7 \times 7 \times 7 = $ _____

c) $2 \times 2 \times 2 \times 2 \times 2 \times 2 \times 2 \times 2 \times 2 \times 2 \times 2 \times 2 = $ _____

d) $8 \times 8 \times 8 \times 8 \times 8 \times 8 \times 8 = $ _____

6 Write each of these numbers in full and find its value.

a) $2^4 = $ _____

b) $3^5 = $ _____

c) $4^4 = $ _____

d) $5^6 = $ _____

Teacher comments

9 Equations and simple functions

Order of operations and algebra

To simplify an algebraic expression, collect the like terms together. Use **BIDMAS** to remind you of the order of operations.

Brackets   **I**ndices   **D**ivision/**M**ultiplication   **A**ddition/**S**ubtraction

Example: Simplify the expression $9p + 7(2p - 3) - p + 11$.

$$9p + 7(2p - 3) - p + 11$$
$$= 9p + 14p - 21 - p + 11 \qquad \text{(expand the brackets)}$$
$$= 9p + 14p - p - 21 + 11 \qquad \text{(collect the like terms together)}$$
$$= 22p - 10 \qquad \text{(simplify by adding like terms)}$$

Exercise 9.1

Simplify the following expressions using the correct order of operations.

1 $2(2a + 4) - a = $ _____

_____

2 $b - 7(4b - 1) + b = $ _____

_____

3 $6(4c - 10) + 7(c - 1) = $ _____

_____

4 $12(8d - 3) - 12(5d + 4) = $ _____

_____

5 $-8(e - 5) + 3(e + 6) = $ _____

_____

6 $-10(4f - 1) + (f - 3) =$ _____

_____

7 $-(7 + 6g) - (-8g + 1) =$ _____

_____

8 $5(7 - h) - 4(h - 1) =$ _____

_____

9 $2i + 7i - 6(i - 9) + 7 =$ _____

_____

10 $8(4j + 2) - (2j - 6) + 9(6j - 1) =$ _____

_____

Indices

A short way to write squares, cubes and other **powers** is to use **indices**.
Example: $a \times a \times a \times a \times a = a^5$

Exercise 9.2

Simplify the following expressions using the correct order of operations.

1 $4^2 + 2(2a + 4) - a =$ _____

_____

2 $b - 7(4b^2 - 1) + b =$ _____

_____

→

3 $6(4c - 10) + 7(c^2 - 1) =$ _____

_____

4 $12(8d - 3) - 12(5d^2 + 4) =$ _____

_____

5 $-8(e - 5) + 3(e^2 + 6) =$ _____

_____

6 $-10(4f^3 - 1) + (f^2 - 3) =$ _____

_____

7 $-(7 + 6g) - (-8g^2 + 1) =$ _____

_____

8 $5(7 - h^3) - 4(h^3 - 1) =$ _____

_____

9 $2i + 7i - 6(i - 9) + 7i^4 =$ _____

_____

10 $8(4j + 2) - (2j^2 - 6) + 9(6j^3 - 1) =$ _____

_____

Further equations

To **solve** an equation to find the value of an unknown (the variable), rearrange the equation so that the variable is on its own on one side of the equation and everything else is on the other side. Remember to keep the equation balanced by always doing the same to both sides.

Example 1: Solve the equation $5(3x - 1) = 7(2x - 5)$

$15x - 5 = 14x - 35$ (expand the brackets)

$x - 5 = -35$ (subtract $14x$ from both sides)

$x = -30$ (add 5 to both sides)

Example 2: Solve the equation $\dfrac{5k}{3} = 10$

$5k = 30$ (multiply both sides by 3)

$k = 6$ (divide both sides by 5)

Exercise 9.3

Solve these equations.

1 a) $a + 14 = 26$ **b)** $2a + 15 = 21$ **c)** $3a + 9 = 42$

$a =$ _____ $a =$ _____ $a =$ _____

2 a) $b - 13 = 4$ **b)** $2b - 16 = 8$ **c)** $3b - 21 = 12$

$b =$ _____ $b =$ _____ $b =$ _____

3 a) $4c = 3c + 2$ **b)** $6c = 7c + 8$ **c)** $8c = 9c + 3$

$c =$ _____ $c =$ _____ $c =$ _____

4 a) $3d = 4d - 2$ **b)** $6d = 4d - 4$ **c)** $8d = 5d - 9$

$d =$ _____ $d =$ _____ $d =$ _____

→

5 **a)** $3e = 4e + 4$ **b)** $9e = 3e + 12$ **c)** $5e = 3e + 8$

$e = \underline{\hphantom{xxxx}}$ $e = \underline{\hphantom{xxxx}}$ $e = \underline{\hphantom{xxxx}}$

6 **a)** $4f = f - 6$ **b)** $5f = f - 24$ **c)** $8f = f - 28$

$f = \underline{\hphantom{xxxx}}$ $f = \underline{\hphantom{xxxx}}$ $f = \underline{\hphantom{xxxx}}$

7 **a)** $15 = g + 9$ **b)** $9 = g - 13$ **c)** $8 = 2g + 12$

$g = \underline{\hphantom{xxxx}}$ $g = \underline{\hphantom{xxxx}}$ $g = \underline{\hphantom{xxxx}}$

8 **a)** $2(h + 1) = 2$ **b)** $3(h + 2) = 9$ **c)** $4(h + 5) = 80$

$h = \underline{\hphantom{xxxx}}$ $h = \underline{\hphantom{xxxx}}$ $h = \underline{\hphantom{xxxx}}$

9 **a)** $4 + 5k = 4k - 8$ **b)** $5k + 7 = 2k + 16$ **c)** $6k - 23 = k + 2$

$k = \underline{\hphantom{xxxx}}$ $k = \underline{\hphantom{xxxx}}$ $k = \underline{\hphantom{xxxx}}$

10 **a)** $5(m - 3) = 4(m - 6)$ **b)** $4(m - 1) = 3(1 - m)$ **c)** $5(m - 4) = 0$

$m = \underline{\hphantom{xxxx}}$ $m = \underline{\hphantom{xxxx}}$ $m = \underline{\hphantom{xxxx}}$

11 **a)** $a + 11 = 4$ **b)** $2a + 19 = 17$ **c)** $3a + 18 = 0$

$a = \underline{\hphantom{xxxx}}$ $a = \underline{\hphantom{xxxx}}$ $a = \underline{\hphantom{xxxx}}$

12 a) $2b - 1 = 1$

b) $4b - 2 = 4$

c) $6b - 3 = 12$

$b = \_\_\_\_$

$b = \_\_\_\_$

$b = \_\_\_\_$

13 a) $5c = 4c + 3$

b) $7c = 5c + 5$

c) $9c = 7c + 9$

$c = \_\_\_\_$

$c = \_\_\_\_$

$c = \_\_\_\_$

14 a) $8d = 4d - 9$

b) $4d = d - 7$

c) $6d = d - 4$

$d = \_\_\_\_$

$d = \_\_\_\_$

$d = \_\_\_\_$

15 a) $e = 2e - 6$

b) $e = 3e - 8$

c) $e = 4e - 10$

$e = \_\_\_\_$

$e = \_\_\_\_$

$e = \_\_\_\_$

16 a) $f = 2f + 6$

b) $f = 3f + 28$

c) $f = 4f + 15$

$f = \_\_\_\_$

$f = \_\_\_\_$

$f = \_\_\_\_$

17 a) $3 = 6g + 7$

b) $9 = 4g - 5$

c) $2 = 2g + 6$

$g = \_\_\_\_$

$g = \_\_\_\_$

$g = \_\_\_\_$

18 a) $9(h + 2) = 8$

b) $4(h + 1) = 12$

c) $12(h + 5) = 66$

$h = \_\_\_\_$

$h = \_\_\_\_$

$h = \_\_\_\_$

➜

47

19 a) $j \div 4 = 4$ **b)** $j \div 5 = 1$ **c)** $j \div 8 = 6$

$j = $ _____ $j = $ _____ $j = $ _____

20 a) $2k \div 3 = 6$ **b)** $3k \div 2 = 9$ **c)** $5k \div 3 = 20$

$k = $ _____ $k = $ _____ $k = $ _____

Constructing and solving equations

You can solve a number problem by forming and solving an equation.

Exercise 9.4

1 I think of a number and add 12. The answer is 15. What is the number?

_____

_____

2 I think of a number and subtract 4. The answer is 6. What is the number?

_____

_____

3 A number times 9 is 63. What is the number?

_____

_____

4 A number divided by 8 is 6. What is the number?

_____

_____

5 I think of a number and add 9. The answer is 20. What is the number?

_____

_____

6 I think of a number and subtract 14. The answer is 36. What is the number?

_____

_____

7 A number times 11 is 121. What is the number?

_____

_____

8 A number divided by 12 is 8. What is the number?

_____

_____

9 I think of a number and add 19. The answer is 34. What is the number?

_____

_____

➜

10 I think of a number and subtract 34. The answer is 26. What is the number?

_____

_____

Teacher comments

10 Constructions

Constructing circles and circle patterns

To **construct** geometric shapes properly, you need a pair of compasses. Leave the construction lines in the final diagram, so that your method of construction is clear.

Exercise 10.1

1   Draw a circle with a radius of 2.5 cm using a pair of compasses.
    Mark the centre as *O*.

2   Construct this circle pattern using a pair of compasses.

Constructing triangles

To construct triangles accurately, you need a ruler, a protractor or angle measurer and a pair of compasses. To construct a right-angled triangle, you need only a ruler and a pair of compasses.

CHAPTER 10

You need to know how to construct a triangle given the length of the base of the triangle and the sizes of the two base angles *or* the lengths of two sides and the size of one angle *or* the lengths of all three sides.

Exercise 10.2

1 **a)** Using only a ruler and a pair of compasses, construct the triangle XYZ, where $XY = 7\,cm$, $XZ = 3\,cm$ and $YZ = 5\,cm$.

b) Measure accurately each of the angles X, Y and Z.

$X =$ _____ $Y =$ _____ $Z =$ _____

2 **a)** Using only a ruler and a pair of compasses, construct the right-angled triangle XYZ.

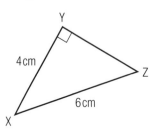

b) Measure accurately the length of the third side.

$YZ =$ _____

Perpendicular bisector and the midpoint

The **perpendicular bisector** of a line segment is at right angles to it and passes through its **midpoint**. To construct a perpendicular bisector, you need a ruler and a pair of compasses.

Exercise 10.3

1   **a)** On the triangle below, construct the perpendicular bisectors of *AC* and *BC*. Label the point of intersection of the two perpendicular bisectors as *O*.

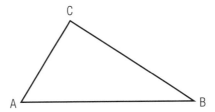

b) Construct an arc that passes through all three vertices *A*, *B* and *C*.

Bisecting an angle

The **bisector** of a angle splits it in half. To construct an angle bisector, you need a ruler and a pair of compasses.

Exercise 10.4

1   Bisect each of the angles below using only a ruler and a pair of compasses.

a)   **b)**

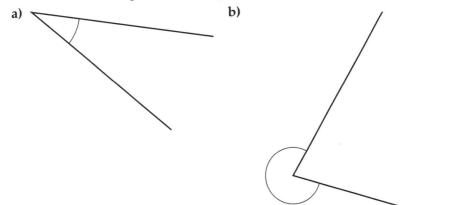

Teacher comments

11 Transformations

The midpoint of a line segment

The **midpoint** of a line segment is the point exactly half way along its length. If the coordinates of the two end points of a line segment are (x_1, y_1) and (x_2, y_2), the coordinates of the midpoint are $\left(\dfrac{x_1 + x_2}{2}, \dfrac{y_1 + y_2}{2} \right)$.

Exercise 11.1

1   Calculate the coordinates of the midpoint M of the line segment joining each of the following pairs of points.

   a) $A = (2, 5)$ and $B = (10, 8)$ **b)** $X = (-6, 4)$ and $Y = (1, -5)$

   $M = \underline{\hphantom{xxxxxxxxx}}$ $M = \underline{\hphantom{xxxxxxxxx}}$

2   A line segment AB has midpoint $M = (3, -6)$ and the coordinates of point A are $(1, -1)$. Calculate the coordinates of point B.

   $B = \underline{\hphantom{xxxxxxxxx}}$

Transformations

In a **reflection**, a **translation** or a **rotation**, the image is exactly the same shape and size as the object.

   If an object is rotated, it is turned about a point known as the **centre of rotation**. Every point on the object is turned by the same amount.

   When transformations are combined, the types of the transformations and the order in which they are carried out affect where the image appears.

Exercise 11.2

1   Draw the image *B* when each of the following objects *A* is rotated by the angle stated about the centre of rotation *O*.

a)

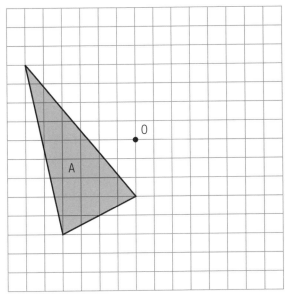

Rotation by 180° about *O*

b)

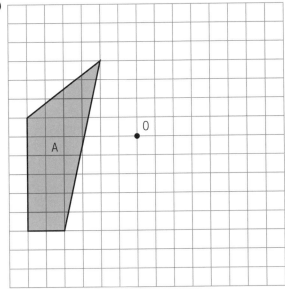

Rotation by 90° anti-clockwise about *O*

CHAPTER 11

2 In each of the following diagrams, the object *P* undergoes two transformations. The first transformation maps *P* on to an image *Q*, the second maps *Q* on to an image *R*. Draw each of the images *Q* and *R*, labelling them clearly.

a)

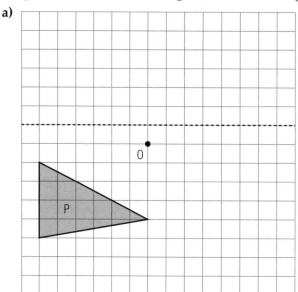

Rotation by 180° about *O*

Reflection in the mirror line

b)

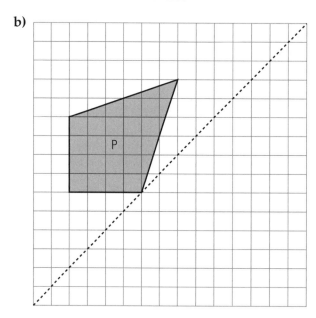

Translation by 4 units to the right and 4 units downwards

Reflection in the mirror line

Teacher comments

Statistical calculations

Averages and the range

The mean, median and mode are three different types of **average**.

$$\text{Mean} = \frac{\text{sum of all the values}}{\text{number of values}}$$

Median = middle value when they are in order of size

Mode = value which occurs most often

The range gives a measure of the **spread** of the data.

Range = difference between the largest and the smallest values

Exercise 12.1

1   The weights (in kilograms) of 12 parcels posted at a post office are recorded below.

   0.56   1.24   0.17   1.33   4.56   0.95   1.05   1.22   0.35   0.66   1.28   1.41

   a) Calculate the mean weight.

   _____

   _____

   b) What is the median weight?

   _____

   _____

   c) What is the modal weight? _____

   d) Calculate the range of the weights. _____

2 As part of an environmental study, a supermarket conducts a survey to see how many plastic shopping bags each customer uses. The frequency table shows the results.

Number of plastic bags	Frequency
0	15
1	18
2	25
3	10
4	5
5	2

a) How many customers were included in the survey? _____

b) How many plastic carrier bags were counted in the survey? _____

c) Calculate the mean number of plastic bags per customer.

_____

d) Calculate the median number of plastic bags per customer.

_____

e) (i) What is the greatest number of plastic bags a customer used?

_____

(ii) What is the smallest number of plastic bags a customer used?

_____

(iii) Calculate the range of the numbers of plastic bags used. _____

CHAPTER 12

Reliability of statistical calculations
Exercise 12.2

1 **a)** Give one advantage of the mean.

_____

   b) Give one disadvantage of the mean.

_____

2 **a)** Give one advantage of the range.

_____

   b) Give one disadvantage of the range.

_____

3 Two companies publish data about how long (in years) their light bulbs last. The table summarises the data.

	Mean	Median	Mode	Range
Company A	3.6	3	3	2
Company B	6	2	1	19

   a) Which company's light bulbs are more consistent? _____
   Explain your answer.

_____

   b) Give a possible reason why the mean result for company B is so much higher than its median or its mode.

_____

_____

c) Both companies want to advertise how long lasting their light bulbs are. Write a short sentence that each company might use in an advertising campaign.

Company A _____

_____

Company B _____

_____

d) Which company's light bulbs do you think last longer? _____ Justify your answer.

_____

Teacher comments

13 Calculations and mental strategies 2

Mental strategies

You can use multiplication facts you know to work out more complicated multiplications.

Exercise 13.1

Multiply the following pairs of numbers in your head, without looking at a multiplication grid or using a calculator.

1 a) $20 \times 6 = $ _____   b) $23 \times 6 = $ _____

   c) $23 \times 60 = $ _____   d) $23 \times 66 = $ _____

2 a) $80 \times 3 = $ _____   b) $81 \times 3 = $ _____

   c) $81 \times 30 = $ _____   d) $81 \times 33 = $ _____

3 a) $70 \times 5 = $ _____   b) $72 \times 5 = $ _____

   c) $72 \times 50 = $ _____   d) $72 \times 55 = $ _____

4 a) $2 \times 30 = $ _____   b) $20 \times 30 = $ _____

   c) $23 \times 30 = $ _____   d) $23 \times 33 = $ _____

5 a) $40 \times 5 = $ _____   b) $44 \times 5 = $ _____

   c) $44 \times 50 = $ _____   d) $44 \times 55 = $ _____

6 a) $3 \times 80 = $ _____   b) $80 \times 80 = $ _____

   c) $80 \times 83 = $ _____   d) $8 \times 0.83 = $ _____

7 a) $2 \times 33 = $ _____   b) $20 \times 33 = $ _____

   c) $22 \times 33 = $ _____   d) $2.2 \times 3.3 = $ _____

8 **a)** $5 \times 32 =$ _____

b) $50 \times 32 =$ _____

c) $55 \times 32 =$ _____

d) $5.5 \times 3.2 =$ _____

Written methods

Remember to line up the decimal points when you write calculations in columns.

Exercise 13.2

1   Without using a calculator, work out these additions.

a) $23.32 + 2.7$ **b)** $19.09 + 0.6$

_____   _____

c) $1.875 + 23.08$ **d)** $6.4 + 12.67$

_____   _____

e) $10.08 + 2.6$

_____

2   Without using a calculator, work out these calculations.

a) $11 - 7.6 + 2.85$ **b)** $2 - 18.098 + 21.3$

_____   _____

c) $4.6 - 6.8 + 2.409$ **d)** $0.456 - 1 + 0.56$

_____   _____

→

e) $69 - 73.6 + 16.005$

_____

3 Without using a calculator, work out these calculations.

a) $150 - 130.07$ **b)** $8.62 + 0.82 + 100.60$

_____   _____

c) $430 - 56.30 - 233.88$ **d)** $1006.40 + 162.71 - 437.08$

_____   _____

4 An office building has 123 floors. The floors are 3.8 m apart.
A lift goes from floor 32 to the top. How far does it travel?

_____

5 A group of five people have a meal.
Their meals cost $7.50, $6.80, $5.75, $10 and $9.25.

a) What is the total bill?

_____

b) How much change should they get if they each pay $8?

_____

6 A girl is 157 cm tall. She was 1.32 m tall a year earlier.
How much has she grown in the year?

_____

7 A bus is 4.2 m high. A truck is 3.45 m high.
How much taller is the bus than the truck?

_____

8 Five cyclists in a time race travel for 1 hour.
They travel 38.25 km, 23.4 km, 30.07 km, 25.78 km and 20.9 km.
a) How far do they travel altogether?

_____

b) The sixth cyclist makes the total up to 170 km.
How far does he travel?

_____

9 A woman owes $310.40 on her credit card account.
Work out her final balance as a positive or negative number after each of these
amounts has been paid or received.
a) Buy dress $33.50

_____

b) Pay garage bill $452

_____

→

c) Pay credit card bill $654.00

_____

d) Pay electricity bill $82.07

_____

e) Pay for fuel $46.03

_____

Teacher comments

SECTION ③

15 Fractions, decimals and percentages

Fractions and decimals

Fractions deal with a part of a whole. A fraction has two parts:

$$\frac{\text{numerator}}{\text{denominator}}$$

Decimals are another way of writing parts of a whole. To convert a fraction to a decimal, divide the numerator by the denominator.

Example 1: $\frac{2}{5} = 2 \div 5 = 0.4$

Using place value, it is straightforward to write a decimal as a fraction with a denominator of 10, 100, 1000, ... Then simplify the fraction if possible.

Example 2: $0.45 = \frac{45}{100} = \frac{9}{20}$

To compare and order fractions, either convert them to equivalent fractions with the same denominator or change them to decimals.

Exercise 15.1

1   Convert each of the following fractions into a decimal by dividing the numerator by the denominator.

a) $\frac{1}{4} =$ _____

b) $\frac{3}{4} =$ _____

c) $\frac{1}{5} =$ _____

d) $\frac{3}{5} =$ _____

e) $\frac{3}{10} =$ _____

f) $\frac{7}{10} =$ _____

g) $\frac{3}{20} =$ _____

h) $\frac{13}{20} =$ _____

i) $\frac{2}{25} =$ _____

j) $\frac{7}{40} =$ _____

→

2 Convert each of the following decimals to a fraction in its simplest form.

a) 0.1 = _____ **b)** 0.7 = _____

c) 0.4 = _____ **d)** 0.8 = _____

e) 0.25 = _____ **f)** 1.75 = _____

g) 0.85 = _____ **h)** 7.35 = _____

i) 0.01 = _____ **j)** 0.05 = _____

3 Write the fractions in question 1 in order, smallest first.

_____

Calculating with fractions

To work out a **fraction of an amount**, look at the denominator of the fraction to see how many equal parts the amount is split into. Simplify your answer if possible.

Example 1: $\frac{1}{5}$ of $33 = 33 \div 5 = 6\frac{3}{5}$

Example 2: $\frac{2}{5}$ of $33 = 6\frac{3}{5} \times 2 = 6 \times 2 + \frac{3}{5} \times 2 = 12 + \frac{6}{5} = 13\frac{1}{5}$

Example 3: $\frac{3}{5}$ of $33 = 6\frac{3}{5} \times 3 = 6 \times 3 + \frac{3}{5} \times 3 = 18 + \frac{9}{5} = 19\frac{4}{5}$

To **add** or **subtract** fractions with different denominators, first change them to equivalent fractions with a common denominator.
It is sometimes easier to change **mixed numbers** to improper fractions first.

Example 4: $9\frac{1}{3} - 7\frac{5}{9} = 9\frac{3}{9} - 7\frac{5}{9} = \frac{84}{9} - \frac{68}{9} = \frac{16}{9} = 1\frac{7}{9}$

To **multiply** a whole number by a fraction, simply multiply the numerator by the whole number.

Example 5: $8 \times \frac{3}{4} = \frac{24}{4} = 6$

Example 6: $12 \times \frac{3}{8} = \frac{36}{8} = 4\frac{4}{8} = 4\frac{1}{2}$

To **divide** by a fraction, remember that multiplying by $\frac{1}{2}$ is the same as dividing by 2.
Similarly, dividing by $\frac{3}{8}$ is the same as multiplying by $\frac{8}{3}$.

Example 7: $7 \div \frac{3}{8} = 7 \times \frac{8}{3} = \frac{56}{3} = 18\frac{2}{3}$

Example 8: $35 \div \frac{7}{8} = 35 \times \frac{8}{7} = \frac{280}{7} = 40$

Exercise 15.2

1 Work out the following.

a) $\frac{1}{8}$ of 74 = _____

b) $\frac{3}{8}$ of 74 = _____

c) $\frac{7}{8}$ of 74 = _____

d) $\frac{1}{12}$ of 150 = _____

e) $\frac{5}{12}$ of 150 = _____

f) $\frac{11}{12}$ of 150 = _____

g) $\frac{1}{8}$ of 246 = _____

h) $\frac{5}{8}$ of 246 = _____

i) $\frac{7}{8}$ of 246 = _____

j) $\frac{1}{11}$ of 90 = _____

k) $\frac{3}{11}$ of 90 = _____

l) $\frac{10}{11}$ of 90 = _____

2 Work out the following amounts exactly.

a) $\frac{3}{8}$ of \$74 = _____

b) $\frac{3}{4}$ of \$90 = _____

c) $\frac{7}{10}$ of \$110.50 = _____

3 Work out the following. Simplify your answers where possible.

a) $\frac{5}{13} + \frac{4}{13} =$ _____

b) $\frac{15}{23} - \frac{11}{23} =$ _____

c) $\frac{3}{4} + \frac{3}{8} =$ _____

d) $\frac{8}{9} - \frac{4}{9} =$ _____

e) $\frac{12}{13} - \frac{5}{13} =$ _____

f) $\frac{3}{4} - \frac{3}{8} =$ _____

g) $9\frac{1}{3} - 7\frac{8}{9} =$ _____

h) $9\frac{1}{2} - 8\frac{3}{4} =$ _____

i) $3\frac{3}{8} - 2\frac{3}{4} =$ _____

4 Work out the following. Simplify your answers where possible.

a) $8 \times \frac{2}{5} =$ _____

b) $15 \times \frac{3}{8} =$ _____

c) $12 \times \frac{4}{9} =$ _____

d) $2 \times \frac{3}{4} =$ _____

e) $5 \times \frac{3}{13}$ _____

f) $3 \times \frac{3}{10}$ _____

5 Work out the following. Simplify your answers where possible.

a) $7 \div \frac{7}{8} =$ _____

b) $14 \div \frac{7}{9} =$ _____

c) $24 \div \frac{12}{13} =$ _____

d) $4 \div \frac{3}{4} =$ _____

e) $18 \div \frac{9}{10} =$ _____

f) $27 \div \frac{3}{4} =$ _____

Percentages

Percentages are another way of writing parts of a whole. A percentage is the number of parts in 100. You should be familiar with the percentage equivalents of simple fractions and decimals.

To calculate a percentage of a quantity, one way is to use the **unitary method**, that is, to work out 1% first.

Example 1: Work out 30% of $2700.
1% of $2700 is $2700 \div 100 = \$27$.
So 30% is $\$27 \times 30 = \$810$.

Alternatively, convert the percentage to a decimal or a fraction and multiply.

To write one quantity as a percentage of another, write the first quantity as a fraction of the second and multiply by 100.

Example 2: What percentage of 120 is 24?
$\frac{24}{120} \times 100 = \frac{1}{5} \times 100 = 20\%$

When calculating a percentage increase or decrease of a quantity, remember that the original amount is 100%.

Example 3: A house bought for $150 000 increases in value by 6%. Calculate its new value.
The new value is 106% of the old value. As a decimal this is 1.06.
The new value is $\$150\,000 \times 1.06 = \$159\,000$.

Exercise 15.3

1 Complete this table.

Fraction	Decimal	Percentage
$\frac{1}{10}$		
$\frac{6}{10}$		
		35%
		45%
	0.12	
$\frac{8}{20}$		
	0.06	
	0.175	
$1\frac{1}{4}$		
$3\frac{3}{4}$		

2 Write the quantities in question 1 in order as decimals, largest first.

_____

3 Work out the following.

a) 10% of 40 _____

b) 25% of 360 _____

c) 20% of 250 _____

d) 12.5% of 40 _____

e) 37.5% of 120 _____

f) 87.5% of 800 _____

g) 24% of 50 _____

h) 50% of 84 _____

i) 84% of 50 _____

j) 40% of 120 _____

k) 4% of 120 _____

l) 4% of 360 _____

m) 10% of 110 _____

n) 30% of 110 _____

o) 300% of 110 _____

p) 90% of 80 _____

q) 8% of 90 _____

r) 900% of 8 _____

4 Write the first quantity as a percentage of the second.

a) 36 out of 72 _____

b) 18 out of 90 _____

c) 5 out of 20 _____

d) 6 out of 60 _____

e) 36 out of 60 _____

f) 54 out of 60 _____

g) 7 out of 70 _____

h) 21 out of 70 _____

i) 49 out of 70 _____

j) 45 out 900 _____

k) 135 out of 900 _____

l) 180 out of 900 _____

5 **a)** A boat priced at $170 000 is increased in price by 20%.
What is the new price?

The new price is _____ of the old price. As a decimal this

is _____

The new price is _____

b) A car priced at $3600 is reduced by 25%.
What is the reduced price?

The new price is_____ of the old price. As a decimal this

is _____

The reduced price is _____ →

c) A furniture shop is having a sale. A chair priced at $400 is reduced by 12.5%. What is the sale price?

The new price is _____ of the old price. As a decimal this

is _____

The sale price is _____

d) A painting is valued at $320 000. At auction, it sells for 37.5% more. What is its selling price?

The selling price is _____ of the valuation. As a decimal this

is _____

The selling price is _____

6 Increase each of the following by the given percentage.

a) 280 by 25% _____

b) 450 by 80% _____

c) 170 by 40% _____

7 Decrease each of the following by the given percentage.

a) 1200 by 75% _____

b) 3300 by 60% _____

c) 1240 by 25% _____

Teacher comments

Sequences, functions and graphs

Sequences

A **sequence** is an ordered set of numbers. Each number in the sequence is called a **term.** The terms of a sequence form a pattern.
There are two types of rule which can be used to describe a sequence:

- a **term-to-term rule** describes how to get from one term to the next
- a **position-to-term rule** describes how to calculate the value of a term from its position in the sequence.

Exercise 16.1

1 These diagrams show the first three patterns in a sequence of growing tile patterns.

a) Draw the next two diagrams in the sequence.

b) Complete this table.

Number of white squares	1	2	3	4	5
Number of grey squares					

c) Describe the term-to-term rule for the number of grey squares.

_____

_____

d) Describe the position-to-term rule linking the number of white squares to the number of grey squares.

_____

_____

e) Explain, using the pattern, why your position-to-term rule works.

_____

_____

f) Use your rule in part **d)** to predict the number of grey squares in a pattern with 100 white squares.

_____

2   These diagrams show the first three patterns in a sequence of growing tile patterns.

a) Draw the next two diagrams in the sequence.

b) Complete this table.

Number of white squares	1	2	3	4	5
Number of grey squares					

c) Describe the term-to-term rule for the number of grey squares.

_____

_____

d) Describe the position-to-term rule linking the number of white squares to the number of grey squares.

_____

_____

e) Explain, using the pattern, why your position-to-term rule works.

_____

_____

f) Use your rule in part **d)** to predict the number of grey squares in a pattern with 100 white squares.

_____

Term-to-term rules

Exercise 16.2

For each of the sequences below:

    a) describe the term-to-term rule

    b) calculate the tenth term.

1 3 6 9 12 15

    a) _____

    b) _____

2 5 11 17 23 29

    a) _____

    b) _____

→

3 10 6 2 −2 −6

a) _____

b) _____

4 3 1.5 0 −1.5 −3

a) _____

b) _____

5 16 8 4 2 1

a) _____

b) _____

6 $\frac{5}{4}$ $\frac{6}{5}$ $\frac{7}{6}$ $\frac{8}{7}$ $\frac{9}{8}$

a) _____

b) _____

The nth term

Using n to represent a term's position in a sequence, the position-to-term rule can be written as an algebraic expression for the value of the **nth term**. It can also be shown as a **mapping**.

Exercise 16.3

1 For each of the sequences below, write down the next two terms and an expression for the nth term.

a) 3 9 15 21 27 ____ ____ nth term = _____

b) −1 3 7 11 15 ____ ____ nth term = _____

c) 0 5 10 15 20 ____ ____ nth term = _____

d) 9 7 5 3 1 _____ _____ nth term = _____

e) $\frac{1}{2}$ $1\frac{1}{2}$ $2\frac{1}{2}$ $3\frac{1}{2}$ $4\frac{1}{2}$ _____ _____ nth term = _____

f) $4\frac{1}{2}$ $2\frac{1}{2}$ $\frac{1}{2}$ $-1\frac{1}{2}$ $-3\frac{1}{2}$ _____ _____ nth term = _____

2   Each of the expressions below gives an expression for the nth term of a sequence.
    Represent the first five terms of each sequence as a mapping.

a) $n - 2$ **b)** $3n - 3$

c) $\frac{1}{2}n + 2$ **d)** $2 - 3n$

Linear graphs

A **line** is made up of an infinite number of points. The **coordinates** of every point
on a straight line all have a common relationship. In other words, the x and y values
follow a pattern. It is this pattern that gives the **equation of the line**.

Exercise 16.4

1   For each of the following straight lines, write in the table the coordinates of five
    of the points on the line and deduce the equation of the line.

a)

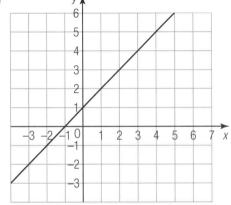

x				
y				

Equation _____

b)

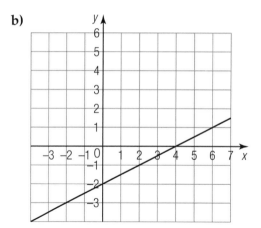

x					
y					

Equation _____

c)

x					
y					

Equation _____

d)

x					
y					

Equation _____

2 By looking at each of the following equations, write whether, if points were plotted, they would produce a horizontal, a vertical or a sloping line.

a) $y = 2x$ _____

b) $y = x - 3$ _____

c) $x = -4$ _____

d) $y = 6$ _____

3 Plot each straight line on the grid provided.
First complete the table to identify the coordinates of some points on the line.

a) $y = x + 3$

x	3	0	-3
y			

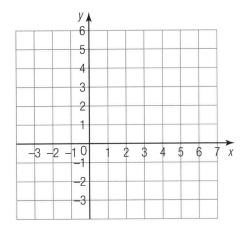

b) $y = 2x$

x	3	0	-3
y			

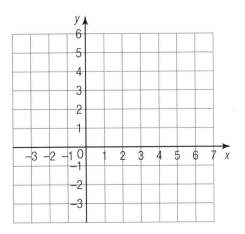

c) $y = x - 3$

x	6	3	0
y			

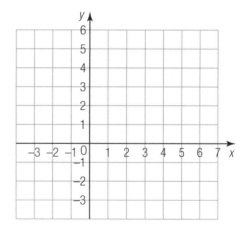

d) $y = -x + 2$

x	3	0	-3
y			

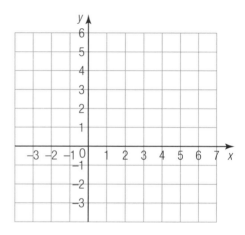

Teacher comments

17 Angle properties

Alternate and corresponding angles

Vertically opposite angles are equal.

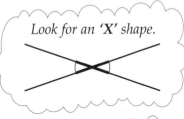

Look for an 'X' shape.

Alternate angles are equal.

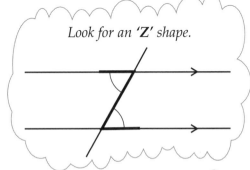

Look for an 'Z' shape.

Corresponding angles are equal.

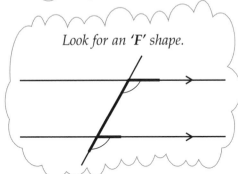

Look for an 'F' shape.

Exercise 17.1

1   Write either 'alternate', 'corresponding' or 'vertically opposite' to complete each of the following sentences.

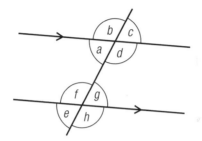

a) Angles *e* and *g* are _____

b) Angles *g* and *c* are _____

c) Angles *h* and *f* are _____

d) Angles *d* and *f* are _____

e) Angles *h* and *d* are _____

2   Calculate the size of each unknown angle in these diagrams. Give reasons for your answers.

a)

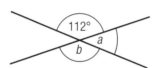

a = _____   _____

b = _____   _____

b)

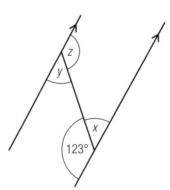

x = _____   _____

$y =$ _____ _____

$z =$ _____ _____

c)

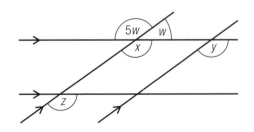

$w =$ _____ _____

$x =$ _____ _____

$y =$ _____ _____

$z =$ _____ _____

d)

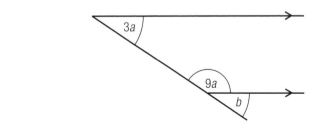

$a =$ _____ _____

$b =$ _____ _____

CHAPTER 17

Angles and triangles

The sum of the three angles of a triangle is always 180°.

An **exterior angle** of a triangle is equal to the sum of the two interior opposite angles.

Exercise 17.2

Calculate the size of each unknown angle in these diagrams.
Give reasons for your answers.

1

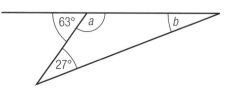

$a = $ _____ _____

$b = $ _____ _____

2

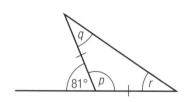

$p = $ _____ _____

$q = $ _____ _____

$r = $ _____ _____

Angles of a quadrilateral

The sum of the four angles of a quadrilateral is always 360°.

Exercise 17.3

Calculate the size of each unknown angle in these diagrams.
Give reasons for your answers.

1

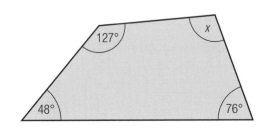

x = _____ _____

2

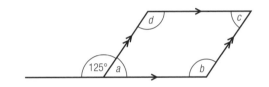

a = _____ _____

b = _____ _____

c = _____ _____

d = _____ _____

Teacher comments

18 Area and volume

The **area** of a plane shape is the amount of two-dimensional (flat) space that it occupies.

Rectangles

Area of a rectangle = length × width

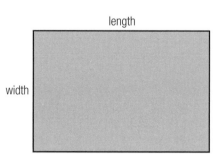

length

width

Exercise 18.1

1 Calculate the area of each of these rectangles.
   Write the units of your answers clearly.

a)   9 cm

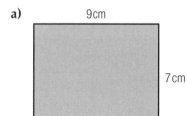

7 cm

b)   5.9 cm

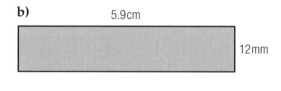

12 mm

Area = _____   Area = _____

2 Calculate the area of each of these rectangles.
   Write the units of your answers clearly.

a) length = 9 cm   width = 8 cm

_____

b) length = 80 cm   width = 12 mm

_____

Triangles

Area of a triangle = $\frac{1}{2} \times$ base length $\times$ perpendicular height

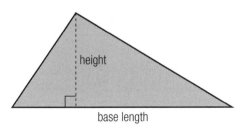

Exercise 18.2

1 Calculate the area of each of these triangles.

a)

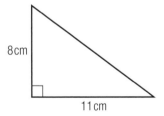

b)

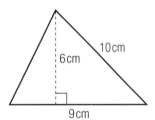

Area = _____   Area = _____

2 Use the formula for the area of a triangle to complete this table.

	Base length	Perpendicular height	Area
a)	4.6 cm	9.4 cm	
b)	10.5 cm		315 cm²
c)		15 cm	27 cm²

3 Calculate the area of each of these shapes. Show your method clearly.

a)

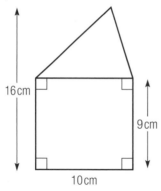

16 cm
9 cm
10 cm

b)

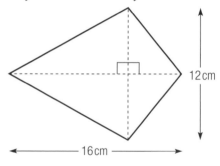

12 cm
16 cm

Area = _____

Area = _____

4 Calculate the area of the shaded region.

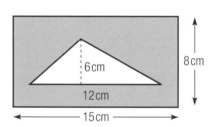

6 cm
12 cm
15 cm
8 cm

Area = _____

Parallelograms and trapeziums

Area of a parallelogram =
base length × perpendicular height

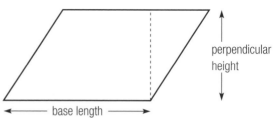

perpendicular height

base length

Area of a trapezium = $\frac{1}{2}(a+b)h$

where a and b are the lengths of
the parallel sides and h is the
shortest distance between them.

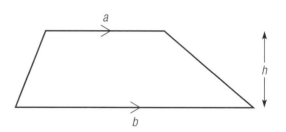

a

h

b

Exercise 18.3

1 Calculate the area of each of these shapes.

a)

9 cm

5 cm

b)

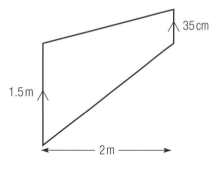

35 cm

1.5 m

2 m

Area = _____   Area = _____

2 Use the formula for the area of a trapezium to complete this table.

	Length *a*	Length *b*	Height	Area
a)	9 cm	10.5 cm	6 cm	
b)	25 cm	55 cm		800 cm²
c)	0.24 m		25 cm	450 cm²

Cuboids

The **volume** of a solid shape is the amount of three-dimensional space that it occupies.

    Volume of a cuboid = length × width × height

The **surface area** of a cuboid is the total area of its six faces.

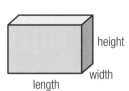

height

width

length

Exercise 18.4

1 The diagram shows a cuboid.

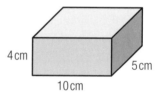

Calculate:

a) its volume _____

b) its surface area. _____

2 The volume of this cuboid is 450 cm³.

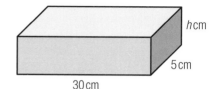

Calculate:

a) its height h _____

b) its surface area. _____

3 The total surface area of this cube is 486 cm².

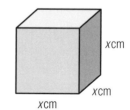

Calculate:

a) the length x of each side _____

b) the volume of the cube. _____

4 The diagram shows a cuboid.

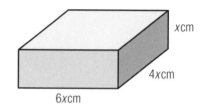

a) Write a formula for the volume of the cuboid in terms of x.

Volume = _____

b) The volume of the cuboid is 648 cm³. Calculate the value of x.

$x =$ _____

c) Calculate the surface area of the cuboid.

Surface area = _____

The circle

The circumference of any circle is given by the formula:

Circumference $= \pi \times$ diameter   or $C = \pi D$

As the diameter is twice the radius, the circumference of a circle can also be given as:

Circumference $= \pi \times 2 \times$ radius   or $C = 2\pi r$

The area of a circle can be calculated using the formula:

Area of a circle $= \pi r^2$

Exercise 18.5

1 Label as many of the different parts of this circle as you can.

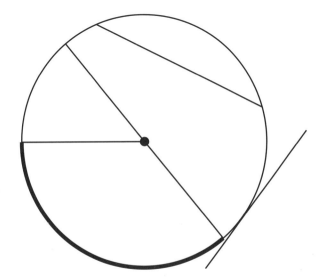

2 Calculate the circumference of each of these circles.
Give your answers correct to two decimal places.

a)

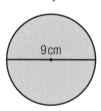

Circumference = _____

b)

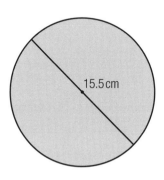

Circumference = _____

⭐ **3** Calculate the perimeter of this semicircle.
Give your answer correct to one decimal place.

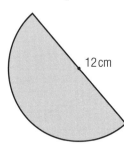

Perimeter = _____

4 Calculate the perimeter of this shape. Show your working clearly.

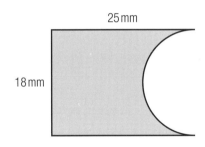

25 mm

18 mm

Perimeter = _____

5 A bicycle wheel has a diameter of 62 cm.

a) Calculate the length of its circumference, correct to one decimal place.

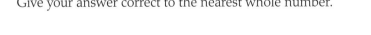

b) How many times will the wheel rotate if a girl rides the bicycle for 3 km?
Give your answer correct to the nearest whole number.

_____

6 Calculate the area of each of these circles.
Give your answers correct to one decimal place.

a)

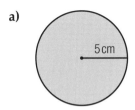

5 cm

b)

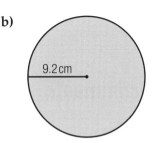

9.2 cm

Area = _____

Area = _____

7 Calculate the area of this shape.
Show your working clearly.

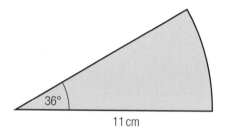

36°

11 cm

Area = _____

8 Calculate the area of the shaded region.
Show your working clearly.

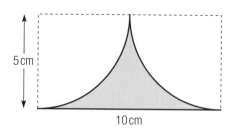

5 cm

10 cm

Area = _____

9 This diagram shows two circular discs
inside a rectangular frame. The discs just
fit inside the frame. Calculate the area of
the rectangle not covered by the discs.

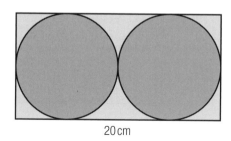

20 cm

Area = _____

Teacher comments

19 Interpreting data and graphs

Data and graphs

It is important to be able not only to present data, but also to **interpret** it. This means understanding what the data shows.

Exercise 19.1

1 The bar chart shows the numbers of people visiting an art gallery each day during one week.

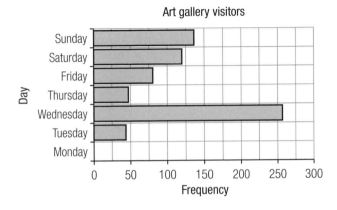

Art gallery visitors

a) Give a possible reason for Monday's data.

_____

b) The museum held a special preview evening for a new exhibition on one of the weekdays. Which weekday is this likely to have been?

_____

Give a reason for your answer. _____

_____

2 A shop manager decides to switch on the heating when the outside temperature falls below 12 °C. The outside temperature is recorded every 2 hours during opening hours on a particular day. The results are shown in the table.

Time	0800	1000	1200	1400	1600	1800	2000	2200
Temperature (°C)	5	10	15	16	17	14	10	7

a) Draw a line graph to show the temperature during the day.

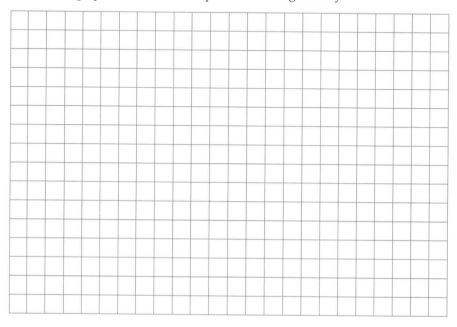

b) Use your graph to estimate the times of day when the outside temperature was 12 °C.

_____

c) Estimate for how long the temperature was higher than 12 °C.

_____

_____.

3   The table shows the age distributions, by percentage of the totals, of two sports
    clubs. One is a golf club; the other is an athletics club.

Age (years)	Percentage	
	Club A	Club B
$0 \leqslant A < 20$	10	55
$20 \leqslant A < 40$	30	35
$40 \leqslant A < 60$	45	8
$60 \leqslant A < 80$	15	2

a) Draw a grouped frequency diagram for each club on the same axes.

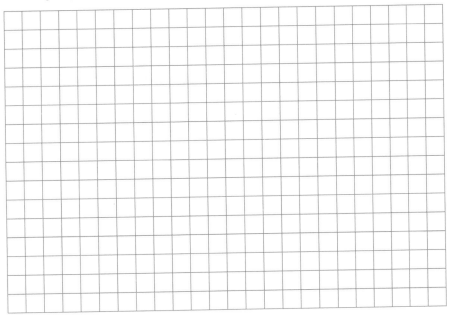

b) Describe the age distribution of each of the clubs.

Club A _____

_____

Club B _____

_____

➡

c) What is the modal age group for each club?

Club A _____

Club B _____

d) In which age group is the median age for each club?

Club A _____

Club B _____

e) Which club is likely to be the athletics club? _____

Give reasons for your answer. _____

_____

Comparing pie charts

Is is easy to compare the data in two pie charts by looking at the sizes of the sectors. But this only tells us about the relative fractions (or percentages) of the two totals. If the totals are different, the actual numbers cannot be compared just by looking at the pie charts and we need to use a common scale, for example percentages.

Exercise 19.2

1   The number of children at two nurseries and their ages are shown in the pie charts.

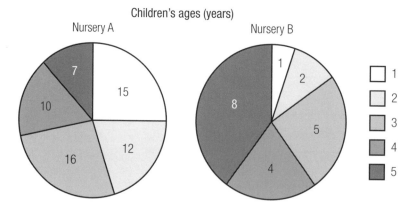

Children's ages (years)

Nursery A   Nursery B

a) What fraction of the children at nursery A are one year old?

_____

b) What fraction of the children at nursery A are two years old?

_____

c) Which nursery has the greater fraction of children who are four years old?

_____

d) Look at the sizes of the sectors of the two pie charts and write a brief comparison of the ages of the children at the two nurseries.

_____

_____

Teacher comments

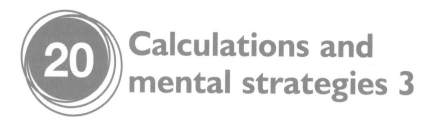

20 Calculations and mental strategies 3

Mental strategies

You can use the laws of arithmetic and inverse operations to work out problems.

Example 1: 25% of $640 = \frac{1}{4} \times 640 = 640 \div 4 = 160$

Example 2: 84% of $50 = \frac{84}{100} \times 50 = 84 \div 2 = 42$

Use **BIDMAS** to remind you of the order of operations in calculations.

Brackets   **I**ndices   **D**ivision/**M**ultiplication   **A**ddition/**S**ubtraction

Example 1: $9 + 7 \times 7 - 8$
$= 9 + 49 - 8$ (multiply first)
$= 50$ (then add and subtract)

Example 2: $25 - (9 + 1) \times 2$
$= 25 - 10 \times 2$ (brackets first)
$= 25 - 20$ (then multiply)
$= 5$ (then subtract)

Exercise 20.1

1 Solve these problems in your head.

   a) A number is doubled and then 9 is subtracted. The answer is 7.
   What is the number?

   _____

   b) A number is halved and then 3 is subtracted. The answer is 3.
   What is the number?

   _____

2 Do these calculations in your head.

   a) $5 + 1 \times 3 - 1 = $ _____   **b)** $5 \times 3 + 5 \times 3 = $ _____

   c) $5 \times 4 - 5 - 4 = $ _____   **d)** $5 + 2 \times 10 - 7 = $ _____

e) $22 - 2 \times 2 \times 4 = $ _____

f) $20 \times (5 + 2) - 125 = $ _____

g) $125 + (12 + 23) \div 5 = $ _____

h) $240 \div (4 + 6) + 30 = $ _____

i) $15 + 15 \times 3 - 15 = $ _____

j) $(18 + 18) \div (12 - 9) = $ _____

3 Write in the missing numbers to make each of these calculations correct.

a) $4 + $ _____ $\times 5 - 20 = 24$

b) $5 \times 7 + 5 \times 4 = $ _____

c) _____ $\times 5 - 25 - 10 = 5$

d) $10 + $ _____ $\times 10 - 50 = 20$

e) $100 - 35 \times 2 \times$ _____ $= 30$

f) $12 \times (1 + $ _____ $) - 90 = 6$

g) _____ $+ (20 + 8) \div 4 = 14$

h) $12 \div (3 + $ _____ $) + 12 = 14$

i) $18 + $ _____ $\times 5 - 18 = 10$

j) $(17 + $ _____ $) \div (9 - 2) = 5$

4 Do these calculations in your head.

a) $\frac{1}{5}$ of $55 = $ _____

b) $\frac{3}{5}$ of $55 = $ _____

c) $\frac{3}{5}$ of $110 = $ _____

d) $\frac{1}{8}$ of $72 = $ _____

e) $\frac{5}{8}$ of $72 = $ _____

f) $\frac{6}{16}$ of $72 = $ _____

g) $\frac{1}{10}$ of $120 = $ _____

h) $\frac{5}{20}$ of $120 = $ _____

i) $\frac{5}{40}$ of $120 = $ _____

j) $\frac{1}{16}$ of $160 = $ _____

k) $\frac{15}{16}$ of $160 = $ _____

l) $\frac{15}{64}$ of $160 = $ _____

m) $\frac{1}{9}$ of $72 = $ _____

n) $\frac{1}{3}$ of $72 = $ _____

o) $\frac{5}{36}$ of $72 = $ _____

→

5   Complete this table.

Fraction	Decimal	Percentage
$\frac{1}{20}$		
	0.15	
		7.5%
$\frac{1}{80}$		
	0.35	
		64%
$\frac{1}{16}$		
	0.55	
		22%
$\frac{3}{100}$		
	0.04	
		6%
$\frac{7}{1000}$		
	0.008	
		9%

6   Work out these percentages in your head.

a) 50% of 34 = _____

b) 34% of 50 = _____

c) 40% of 24 = _____

d) 24% of 40 = _____

e) 8% of 150 = _____

f) 12.5% of 32 = _____

g) 32% of 12.5 = _____

h) 37.5% of 640 = _____

i) 8% of 75 = _____

j) 75% of 160 = _____

Written methods

Most divisions do not give an exact answer. Rather than giving the answer with a fraction or a remainder, you can continue the division and give your answer to a number of decimal places.

Example: Calculate 69 ÷ 8. Give your answer to two decimal places.

```
        8.6 2 5
    8 | 6 9.0 0 0
        6 4
        ‾‾‾
          5 0
          4 8
          ‾‾‾
            2 0
            1 6
            ‾‾‾
              4 0
```

> *Continue the division until the third decimal place so that you can round the answer correctly.*

Therefore 69 ÷ 8 = 8.625 = 8.63 (to two decimal places).

Exercise 20.2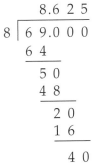

1   Calculate the following divisions. Give your answers to two decimal places.

   a) 59 ÷ 5   **b)** 48 ÷ 7   **c)** 66 ÷ 9

   d) 53 ÷ 6   **e)** 70 ÷ 8   **f)** 55 ÷ 4

   g) 166 ÷ 8   **h)** 125 ÷ 3   **i)** 247 ÷ 7

2   Calculate the following divisions. Give your answers to two decimal places.

   a) 74 ÷ 9   **b)** 57 ÷ 5   **c)** 6 ÷ 7

   d) 28 ÷ 3   **e)** 67 ÷ 6   **f)** 233 ÷ 4

   g) 11 ÷ 8   **h)** 14.34 ÷ 9   **i)** 8 ÷ 7

3   Eight identical cars just fit end to end on a ferry. The total length of the car deck is 43 m. What is the length of each car? Give your answer to two decimal places.

→

4   A wall is 2.5 m high. It is made of seven rows of identical concrete blocks. How high is each row of blocks? Give your answer to three decimal places.

Teacher comments

Ratio and proportion

A **ratio** shows the relative sizes of two numbers, similar to a **fraction**.
If two ratios are equivalent then they are **in proportion**.

Example 1: $8:12$ and $48:72$ are equivalent (in proportion), as 8 is two-thirds of 12 and 48 is two-thirds of 72.

Example 2: $\frac{3}{7} = \frac{12}{28}$ because $3 \times 4 = 12$ and $7 \times 4 = 28$. The top and bottom of the fraction have both increased by a factor of 4.

A **percentage** is a ratio of a number to 100. A percentage can be converted to an equivalent fraction or decimal.

Example 3: 20% is the same as the ratio of 20 to 100, or the fraction $\frac{20}{100} = \frac{1}{5}$.

Example 4: $16\% = \frac{16}{100} = 0.16$

Example 5: $\frac{18}{20} = \frac{90}{100}$ (multiplying top and bottom by 5), so $\frac{18}{20}$ is equivalent to 90%.

Like fractions, ratios can be simplified.

Example 6: 2 litres : 750 ml = 2000 ml : 750 ml = 2000 : 750 = 8 : 3

Exercise 22.1

1   Write either 'yes' or 'no' to indicate whether each of the following pairs of ratios are in proportion.

a) 1 to 5 and 5 to 25 _____   b) 2 to 6 and 6 to 18 _____

c) 5 to 25 and 25 to 125 _____   d) 9 to 6 and 80 to 120 _____

e) 7 to 21 and 22 to 62 _____   f) 19 to 38 and 38 to 19 _____

g) 5 to 10 and 111 to 222 _____ **h)** 6 to 36 and 5 to 25 _____

i) 10 to 13 and 13 to 10 _____ **j)** 5 to 25 and 25 to 15 _____

2 Complete these pairs of equivalent fractions.

a) $\dfrac{18}{12}$ and $\dfrac{6}{}$ **b)** $\dfrac{72}{81}$ and $\dfrac{24}{}$

c) $\dfrac{35}{40}$ and $\dfrac{}{16}$ **d)** $\dfrac{4}{5}$ and $\dfrac{}{50}$

e) $\dfrac{30}{40}$ and $\dfrac{9}{}$ **f)** $\dfrac{54}{72}$ and $\dfrac{3}{}$

g) $\dfrac{96}{144}$ and $\dfrac{12}{}$ **h)** $\dfrac{3}{27}$ and $\dfrac{9}{}$

i) $\dfrac{400}{1000}$ and $\dfrac{40}{}$ **j)** $\dfrac{8}{18}$ and $\dfrac{24}{}$

3 Complete these sets of equivalent fractions and percentages.

a) $\dfrac{48}{144} = \dfrac{1}{}$ **b)** $\dfrac{25}{45} = \dfrac{}{18}$

c) $\dfrac{14}{20} = \underline{\hphantom{00}}\%$ **d)** $\dfrac{22}{200} = \underline{\hphantom{00}}\%$

e) $\dfrac{13}{50} = \underline{\hphantom{00}}\%$ **f)** $\dfrac{16}{48} = \dfrac{1}{}$

g) $\dfrac{80}{250} = \dfrac{}{100} = \underline{\hphantom{00}}\%$ **h)** $\dfrac{20}{250} = \dfrac{}{1000} = \underline{\hphantom{00}}\%$

i) $\dfrac{56}{400} = \dfrac{}{100} = \underline{\hphantom{00}}\%$ **j)** $\dfrac{70}{2000} = \dfrac{}{200} = \underline{\hphantom{00}}\%$

4 Write either 'yes' or 'no' to indicate whether each of the following are equivalent (in proportion).

a) $\dfrac{2}{10}$ 0.2 20% _____ **b)** $\dfrac{1}{4}$ 0.4 40% _____

c) $\dfrac{1}{8}$ 0.125 12.5% _____ **d)** $\dfrac{1}{3}$ 0.33 33% _____

e) $\dfrac{4}{50}$ 0.8 8% _____ **f)** $\dfrac{3}{8}$ 0.375 37.5% _____

g) $\dfrac{2}{3}$ 0.66 66% _____ **h)** $\dfrac{19}{100}$ 0.19 19% _____

i) $\dfrac{3}{20}$ 0.15 15% _____ **j)** 5 5.0 500% _____

5   Simplify these ratios.

a) $12:16 =$ _____

b) $36:60 =$ _____

c) $18:45 =$ _____

d) 1 hour 20 minutes : 4 hours = _____

e) $5\,kg:1250\,g =$ _____

f) $16\,m:150\,cm =$ _____

g) 28 litres to $3000\,ml =$ _____

h) $7 to 70 cents = _____

i) 12 hours to 4 days = _____

j) 40 weeks to 5 years = _____

Direct proportion

You can use the **unitary method** to solve problems involving direct proportion.

Example: A machine makes 200 boxes in 4 hours.
How many boxes does it make in 24 hours?
The machine makes $200 \div 4 = 50$ boxes in 1 hour so it makes
$50 \times 24 = 1200$ boxes in 24 hours.

Exercise 22.2

Use the unitary method to solve these problems.

1   A cooker uses 6 units of electricity in 80 minutes.
How many units does it use in 2 hours?

_____

_____

→

2 A machine produces 100 pens in 90 seconds.
How many does it produce in 6 hours?

_____

_____

3 A baker makes 18 cakes in a 12-hour day.
How many does she make in a 60-hour week?

_____

_____

4 A combine harvester produces 36 tonnes of grain in 24 hours.
How many tonnes does it produce in 54 hours?

_____

_____

5 A machine puts tar on a road at the rate of 48 metres in 1 hour.

a) How long does it take to cover 1 km of road?

_____

_____

b) How many metres of road does it cover in 8 hours?

_____

_____

6 The ratio of girls to boys in a class is 42 : 35.
There are 18 girls. How many boys are there?

_____

_____

7   Sand and gravel are mixed in the ratio 44:33 to make ballast.
    80 kg of sand is used. How much gravel is used?

    _____

    _____

8   A paint mix uses blue and white in the ratio 0.75:2.5.
    6.6 litres of blue paint are used. How much white paint is used?

    _____

    _____

9   A necklace has green and blue beads in the ratio 1:1.5.
    There are 24 green beads on the necklace. How many blue beads are there?

    _____

    _____

Dividing a quantity in a given ratio

To divide a quantity in a given ratio, first work out how many parts the total quantity represents. Then use the unitary method.

Example: A piece of rope is 120 cm long. It is cut into two pieces in the ratio 7:3.
             How long is each piece?
             The ratio of 7:3 means you need to consider the rope as 7 + 3 = 10 parts.
             10 parts are 120 cm, so 1 part is 120 cm ÷ 10 = 12 cm.
             7 parts are 7 × 12 cm = 84 cm and 3 parts are 3 × 12 cm = 36 cm.

Exercise 22.3

1   Divide 750 in the ratio 9:6.

    _____

    _____

→

2   Divide 288 in the ratio 100 : 200.

_____

_____

3   Divide 10 kg in the ratio 12 : 18.

_____

_____

4   Divide 1 minute in the ratio 15 : 21.

_____

_____

5   Divide 8 m in the ratio 9 : 39.

_____

_____

6   Divide 45 km in the ratio 42 : 58.

_____

_____

7   Divide 4 hours in the ratio 25 : 15.

_____

_____

8 Divide 2 kg in the ratio 27:63.

_____

_____

9 Divide 3 litres in the ratio 49:35.

_____

_____

10 Divide 1 m in the ratio 10:15:25.

_____

_____

11 Divide 70 litres in the ratio 6:12:24.

_____

_____

12 Divide 1 hour in the ratio 15:18:27.

_____

_____

13 Divide 2 km in the ratio 24:64:72.

_____

_____

→

14 Divide 9 kg in the ratio 30 : 140 : 190.

_____

_____

15 Divide $75 in the ratio 27 : 45 : 63.

_____

_____

Teacher comments

Formulae and substitution

Substitution into an expression

We can replace the letters in expressions by numbers. This is called **substituting** the numbers for the letters.

Example: Calculate the value of the expressions below when $a = 4$ and $b = 7$.

    a) $a + b$

        $= 4 + 7$

        $= 11$

    b) $a + 2b$

        $= 4 + 2 \times 7$

        $= 4 + 14$

        $= 18$

Exercise 23.1

Calculate the value of the expressions below when $a = 5$, $b = 4$, $c = -3$ and $d = -2$.

1 $a + b + c$ _____

2 $a - b - c$ _____

3 $a + b - c$ _____

4 $a + b - c - d$ _____

5 $8a$ _____

6 $-5b$ _____

7 $7c$ _____

8 $-3d$ _____

9 $a + 4b + c + 3d$ _____

10 $3a - 4b + c - 3d$ _____

11 $a - 4b - c - 5d$ _____

➜

12 $4a + 4b - 4c - 4d$ _____

13 $4(a + b - c - d)$ _____

14 a^2 _____

15 b^2 _____

16 c^2 _____

17 d^2 _____

18 $a^2 + b^2$ _____

19 $a^2 - b^2$ _____

20 $a^2 - b^2 + c^2 - d^2$ _____

21 a^3 _____

22 $b^3 - b^2$ _____

23 $c^3 - c^2$ _____

24 $d^3 - 2a$ _____

25 $d^3 - c^3$ _____

Substitution into a formula

We can substitute known values for the letters in a formula to find an unknown value.

Example: If an object has starting velocity u and acceleration a, the formula $v = u + at$ can be used to find its final velocity v after time t.
Find the final velocity when $u = 5$, $a = 2$ and $t = 5$.
$v = 5 + 2 \times 5$
$v = 5 + 10$
$v = 15$

Exercise 23.2

1   Given the formula $v = u + at$, find the value of v when:
   a) $u = 0$, $a = 6$ and $t = 4$

   _____

   b) $u = 10$, $a = 9$ and $t = 3$

   _____

   c) $u = 50$, $a = 10$ and $t = 20$

   _____

   d) $u = 75$, $a = -6$ and $t = 10$

   _____

   e) $u = 45$, $a = -9$ and $t = 5$

   _____

2   Given the formula $s = ut + \frac{1}{2}at^2$, find the value of s when:
   a) $u = 0$, $t = 1$ and $a = 4$

   _____

   b) $u = 10$, $t = 2$ and $a = 12$

   _____

   c) $u = 20$, $t = 3$ and $a = 8$

   _____

   d) $u = 12$, $t = 5$ and $a = 12$

   _____

   e) $u = 1000$, $t = 0$ and $a = 10$

   _____

→

Converting between temperature scales

The formula for converting a temperature in degrees Celsius (C) into a temperature in degrees Fahrenheit (F) is

$$F = \frac{9}{5}C + 32$$

The formula for converting from degrees Fahrenheit to degrees Celsius is

$$C = \frac{5}{9}(F - 32)$$

Example 1:   Convert 25°C to degrees Fahrenheit.
$F = \frac{9}{5} \times 25 + 32 = 9 \times 5 + 32 = 45 + 32 = 77$
Therefore 25 °C is equivalent to 77 °F.

Example 2:   Convert 95 °F to degrees Celsius.
$C = \frac{5}{9}(95 - 32) = \frac{5}{9} \times 63 = 5 \times 7 = 35$
Therefore 95 °F is equivalent to 35 °C.

Exercise 23.3

1   Convert these temperatures to degrees Fahrenheit.

a) 5°C _____

b) 10°C _____

c) −20°C _____

d) 22.5°C _____

e) 37.5°C _____

2   Convert these temperatures to degrees Celsius.

a) 212°F _____

b) 176°F _____

c) 23°F _____

d) −4°F _____

e) −148°F _____

Using substitution to form and solve an equation

If the unknown value is not on its own on the left-hand side of a formula, when you substitute the known values you will be left with an equation to solve.

Example: Use the formula $v = u + at$ to find the value of u when $v = 35$, $a = 2$ and $t = 10$.

$$35 = u + (2 \times 10)$$
$$35 = u + 20$$
$$35 - 20 = u$$
$$u = 15$$

Exercise 23.4

In each of these questions, the values of three of v, u, a and t are given.
Use the formula $v = u + at$ to form an equation and find the missing value.

1 $v = 56$, $a = 7$ and $t = 6$

$u = $ _____

2 $v = 72$, $a = 5$ and $t = 9$

$u = $ _____

3 $v = 200$, $a = 18$ and $t = 10$

$u = $ _____

4 $v = 96$, $t = 7$ and $u = 12$

$a = $ _____

5 $v = 500$, $t = 20$ and $u = 20$

$a = $ _____

Teacher comments

Enlargement and scale drawing

Enlargement

An **enlargement** is a transformation in which the final image usually has a different position and size to the original object. The lengths in the object are all multiplied by the same amount to give the image lengths. The number which multiplies the lengths is called the **scale factor of enlargement**.

Exercise 24.1

1 In each of the diagrams below, shape B is bigger than shape A.

   a) Decide whether B is an enlargement of A.

   b) If B is an enlargement of A, calculate the scale factor of enlargement.

   a) 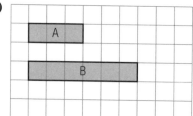   **b)**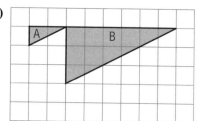

   Enlargement? _____   Enlargement? _____

   Scale factor = _____   Scale factor = _____

2 Enlarge each of the objects below by the given scale factor of enlargement.
   a)

   Scale factor of enlargement 2

b)

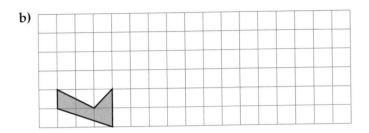

Scale factor of enlargement 3

Centre of enlargement

The mathematical way to describe an enlargement is to give both the scale factor of enlargement and the position of the **centre of enlargement**.

Exercise 24.2

1 Enlarge each of the objects below by the given scale factor of enlargement and from the centre of enlargement O.

a)

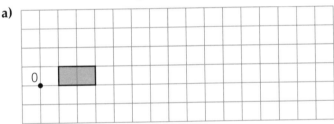

Scale factor of enlargement 3

b)

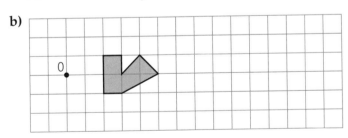

Scale factor of enlargement 2

2   In each of the diagrams below, the larger shape is an enlargement of the smaller
    one from the centre of enlargement O. Calculate the scale factor of enlargement
    in each case.

a)

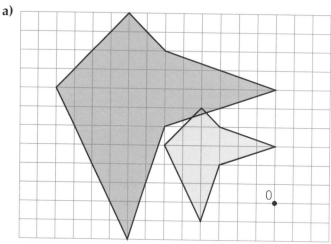

    Scale factor = _____

b)

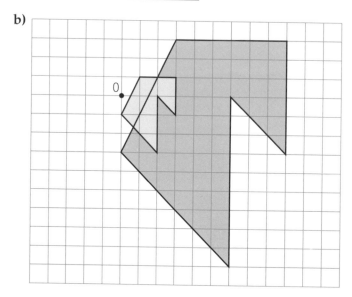

    Scale factor = _____

Scale drawings

In a **scale drawing**, all the lengths are changed by the same scale factor. The scale is shown using a ratio. For example, a scale of 1:50 means that 1 cm on the diagram represents 50 cm in real life.

Exercise 24.3

1 Calculate the actual length (in metres) represented by each of these lengths on a scale drawing. The scale of each diagram is given in brackets.

   a) 12 cm   (1:40)

   _____

   b) 3.5 cm   (1:80)

   _____

   c) 25 mm   (1:500)

   _____

2 Calculate the length (in centimetres) that represents each of these actual lengths on a scale drawing. The scale of each diagram is given in brackets.

   a) 75 m   (1:100)

   _____

   b) 200 m   (1:400)

   _____

   c) 350 cm   (1:40)

   _____

➜

3 In each of these pairs of lengths, the first is the length on a scale drawing and the second is the corresponding length in real life. Calculate the scale in each case.

a) 12 cm   1200 cm

_____

b) 15 cm   6 m

_____

c) 2 cm   30 m

_____

4 This diagram shows the plan of a room drawn to a scale of 1:40.

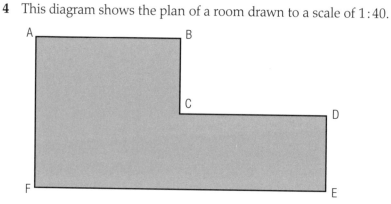

a) Measure the length *AF* in centimetres. _____

b) Calculate the actual length *AF* in the room.

_____

c) Measure the length *CD* in centimetres. _____

d) Calculate the actual length *CD* in the room.

_____

e) Measure the length *CF* in centimetres. _____

f) Calculate the actual length *CF* in the room.

_____

5 This diagram shows the plan of a school playing field. The scale used is 1:2000.

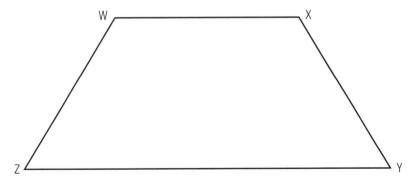

a) Measure the length *WX* in centimetres. _____

b) What is the actual length of *WX*? Give your answer in metres.

_____

c) Measure the length *YZ* in centimetres. _____

d) What is the actual length of *YZ*? Give your answers in metres.

_____

e) Mark out a football pitch 100 m long and 70 m wide on the plan of the field above.

Teacher comments

Nets and surface area

Nets

A **net** is a two-dimensional representation of the faces of a three-dimensional object. By folding the net up, the three-dimensional object is created.

Exercise 25.1

Sketch at least two different nets for each of the following three-dimensional objects. Label the dimensions of each part of your diagrams.

1

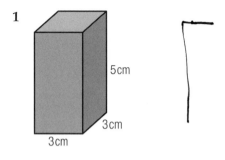

a cuboid

2

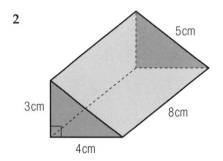

a triangular prism

Surface area of three-dimensional shapes

The **surface area** of a three-dimensional shape is the total area of all of its faces.

Exercise 25.2

1   Calculate the surface area of the cuboid in question 1 of Exercise 25.1.

_____

_____

2   Calculate the surface area of the triangular prism in question 2 of Exercise 25.1.

_____

_____

Teacher comments

26 Probability

Revision

The probability of an event happening must have a value between 0 and 1.
If the probability of an event happening is p, then the probability of the event not happening is $1 - p$.

Exercise 26.1

1 a) An ordinary six-sided dice is rolled. Calculate the probability:

      (i) of getting a 1 or a 2 _____

      (ii) of not getting a 1 or a 2 _____

  b) What do you notice about your answers in part a)?

    _____

2 A coloured spinner is spun. It has three colours: red, blue and yellow.
If $P(\text{red}) = \frac{1}{6}$ and $P(\text{blue}) = \frac{1}{6}$, calculate:

  a) P(yellow) _____

  b) P(not red) _____

  c) P(not blue) _____

Combined events

Combined events are about probability involving two or more events.

Exercise 26.2

1   a) Two four-sided dice are rolled. Complete the two-way table to show all the
        possible combinations.

		Dice 1			
		1	2	3	4
Dice 2	1			3, 1	
	2				
	3				
	4				

   b) Write down the probability:

   (i)   of getting a double 2 _____

   (ii) of not getting a double 2 _____

   (iii) of getting any double _____

   (iv) of getting a total score of 5 _____

   (v)   of not getting a total score of 5 _____

   (vi) of getting a total score of 10 _____

   →

2 A boy rolls an ordinary six-sided dice and spins an eight-sided spinner.
The colours on the spinner are white, red, orange, yellow, green, blue, indigo
and violet.

a) Draw a two-way table to show all the possible outcomes.

b) Write down the probability:

    (i)   of getting green on the spinner _____

    (ii)   of getting 3 on the dice _____

    (iii) of getting green on the spinner or 3 on the dice _____

    (iv) of getting green on the spinner and 3 on the dice _____

    (v)   of getting red, white or blue on the spinner _____

    (vi) of getting a multiple of 2 on the dice _____

(vii) of getting red, white or blue on the spinner or a multiple of 2 on the dice

_____

(viii) of getting red, white or blue on the spinner and a multiple of 2 on the

dice _____

Experimental and theoretical probabilities

The theoretical probability and the experimental probability need not be the same.

Exercise 26.3

1 a) What is the theoretical probability of getting a head when a fair coin is

flipped? _____

b) Find a coin that you think is fair.

(i) Flip the coin five times and record the results.
What is the experimental probability of getting a head?

_____

(ii) Flip the coin another five times and record the results.
Using all ten results, what is the experimental probability of getting
a head?

_____

(iii) Flip the coin another ten times and record the results.
Using all 20 results, what is the experimental probability of getting
a head?

_____

→

(iv) Flip the coin another 30 times and record the results.

Using all 50 results, what is the experimental probability of getting a head?

_____

c) Which of the results from part **b)** gives the most accurate estimate of the experimental probability of getting a head with your coin?

_____

Explain your answer. _____

_____

d) Do you think your coin is fair? _____

Explain your answer. _____

_____

Teacher comments

Calculations and mental strategies 4

Mental strategies

Exercise 27.1

Do these questions in your head, without using a calculator.

1   a) $9 \times 9 =$ _____

   b) $7 \times 9 =$ _____

   c) $14 \times 9 =$ _____

   d) $7 \times 3 =$ _____

   e) $50 \times 3 =$ _____

2   a) $64 \div 8 =$ _____

   b) $18 \div 9 =$ _____

   c) $36 \div 3 =$ _____

   d) $99 \div 9 =$ _____

   e) $36 \div 4 =$ _____

→

3 Without doing any division, complete the following table.

	Number	Divisible by 5?	Divisible by 6?	Divisible by 9?
	702	✗	✓	✓
a)	1305			
b)	7340			
c)	840			
d)	145			
e)	367			
f)	3005			
g)	2736			
h)	3963			
i)	3333			
j)	5412			

4 **a)** $\frac{3}{2} \times 6 =$ _____

   b) $\frac{3}{2} \times 10 =$ _____

   c) $\frac{4}{5} \times 25 =$ _____

   d) $\frac{4}{5} \times 55 =$ _____

   e) $\frac{7}{8} \times 24 =$ _____

5 **a)** $\frac{8}{3} \div 4 =$ _____

   b) $\frac{4}{5} \div 4 =$ _____

   c) $\frac{16}{5} \div 8 =$ _____

   d) $\frac{7}{8} \div 7 =$ _____

   e) $\frac{8}{9} \div 8 =$ _____

6 **a)** $11 \times 9 =$ _____

    b) $11 \times 0.9 =$ _____

    c) $1.1 \times 9 =$ _____

    d) $1.1 \times 0.09 =$ _____

    e) $0.11 \times 0.9 =$ _____

7 **a)** $48 \div 3 =$ _____

    b) $4.8 \div 3 =$ _____

    c) $4.8 \div 0.3 =$ _____

    d) $2.4 \div 0.3 =$ _____

    e) $4.8 \div 0.6 =$ _____

✪ 8 Complete these so that the ratios in each pair are equivalent (in proportion).

    a) 2 to 3 and 6 to _____

    b) 8 to 9 and _____ to 27

    c) 12 to _____ and 3 to 12

    d) 8 to 7 and _____ to 49

    e) 1 to 5 and 5 to _____

    f) 6 to 7 and _____ to 42

    g) 8 to 1 and 12 to _____

    h) 2 to 5 and _____ to 50

    i) 3 to 10 and _____ to 15

    j) 4 to 3 and _____ to 51

9 **a)** Three text messages cost 5 cents to send. How much do 150 cost?

_____

   b) Five identical oil tanks hold 6000 litres. How much do two tanks hold?

_____

Written methods

You can use place value to multiply or divide a number by a decimal.

Example 1: $6.54 \times 3 = 19.62$ so $6.54 \times 0.3 = 1.962$ and $6.54 \times 0.03 = 0.1962$

Example 2: $8.73 \div 3 = 2.91$ so $8.73 \div 0.3 = 2.91 \times 10 = 29.1$ and $8.73 \div 0.03 = 2.91 \times 100 = 291$

Exercise 27.2

Without using a calculator, work out the multiplications in questions 1–10.

1 **a)** 7.32×2 **b)** 7.32×0.2 **c)** 7.32×0.02

   _____   _____   _____

2 **a)** 5.43×6 **b)** 5.43×0.6 **c)** 5.43×0.06

   _____   _____   _____

3 **a)** 9.87×3 **b)** 9.87×0.3 **c)** 9.87×0.03

   _____   _____   _____

4 **a)** 10.5×4 **b)** 10.5×0.4 **c)** 10.5×0.04

   _____   _____   _____

5 **a)** 0.88×5 **b)** 0.88×0.5 **c)** 0.88×0.05

   _____   _____   _____

6 **a)** 11.35×6 **b)** 11.35×0.6 **c)** 11.35×0.06

————   ————   ————

7 **a)** 0.44×7 **b)** 0.44×0.7 **c)** 0.44×0.07

————   ————   ————

8 **a)** 12.1×8 **b)** 12.1×0.8 **c)** 12.1×0.08

————   ————   ————

9 **a)** 4.33×9 **b)** 4.33×0.9 **c)** 4.33×0.09

————   ————   ————

10 a) 5.3×2 **b)** 5.3×0.2 **c)** 5.3×0.02

————   ————   ————

Without using a calculator, work out the divisions in questions 11–20.

11 a) $7.71 \div 3$ **b)** $7.71 \div 0.3$ **c)** $7.71 \div 0.03$

————   ————   ————

12 a) $0.74 \div 2$ **b)** $0.74 \div 0.2$ **c)** $0.74 \div 0.02$

————   ————   ————

13 a) $4.26 \div 3$ **b)** $4.26 \div 0.3$ **c)** $4.26 \div 0.03$

————   ————   ————

14 a) $4.44 \div 4$ **b)** $4.44 \div 0.4$ **c)** $4.44 \div 0.04$

————   ————   ————

15 a) $18.8 \div 5$ **b)** $18.8 \div 0.5$ **c)** $18.8 \div 0.05$

———————   ———————   ———————

16 a) $24.36 \div 6$ **b)** $24.36 \div 0.6$ **c)** $24.36 \div 0.06$

———————   ———————   ———————

17 a) $43.4 \div 7$ **b)** $43.4 \div 0.7$ **c)** $43.4 \div 0.07$

———————   ———————   ———————

18 a) $40.08 \div 8$ **b)** $40.08 \div 0.8$ **c)** $40.08 \div 0.08$

———————   ———————   ———————

19 a) $72.45 \div 9$ **b)** $72.45 \div 0.9$ **c)** $72.45 \div 0.09$

———————   ———————   ———————

20 a) $0.15 \div 3$ **b)** $0.15 \div 0.3$ **c)** $0.15 \div 0.03$

———————   ———————   ———————

Without using a calculator, work out the calculations in questions 21–30.
Think carefully where to place the decimal point.

21 a) 8.13×3 **b)** 8.13×0.03

———————   ———————

22 a) $8.13 \div 3$ **b)** $8.13 \div 0.03$

———————   ———————

23 a) 7.9×5 **b)** 7.9×0.05

———————   ———————

24 a) $7.9 \div 5$ **b)** $7.9 \div 0.05$

———————   ———————

25 a) 3.33×7 **b)** 3.33×0.07

_____   _____

26 a) $3.15 \div 7$ **b)** $3.15 \div 0.07$

_____   _____

27 a) $64 \div 8$ **b)** $64 \div 0.08$

_____   _____

28 a) 5×8 **b)** 8×0.005

_____   _____

29 a) 9×7 **b)** 7×0.09

_____   _____

30 a) $11 \div 2$ **b)** $11 \div 0.02$

_____   _____

Teacher comments